Acknow

This book became reality partly due to the unselfish and devoted efforts of Suzie Jankov Mazella, daughter of my friend Vito, and Linda Hristovski, wife of my friend Risto, who are both computer wizards. Then my son, Gregory, took charge with final editing and layout. To all three, my humble thanks and appreciation.

Chapter I   The Balkans, Post World War II

The big guns stopped delivering incalculable death to humanity. The screeching planes stopped carpet-bombing the German cities. The armies went back to their respective homelands, many of them maimed physically and emotionally for life, and millions never making it home, killed on the battlefields, or captured in prisons or concentration camps. But the stagnated air, saturated with gunpowder and human blood, started to dissipate and a few rays of sun penetrated through, bringing some hope to the shell-shattered, demoralized, and exhausted populace. People began the slow, difficult process of trying to pick up the pieces and start their lives anew.

However, many regions of unlucky people who found themselves under the Russian "liberation" powers, found their lives taking a completely different turn. After succumbing to the Communist weight, brutal coercion, propaganda, physical brutality and military actions, many Eastern European countries found themselves in precarious situations. But this was not enough for Russia, and they started clandestine action in Greece to impose Communism upon them, upsetting the status quo. By the beginning of 1948, Greece was fully involved in a civil war.

The revolutionary forces, consisting mostly of rag-tag personalities, persuaded by the perceived benefits of the upcoming communist system, and many forcibly coerced by the pressures and promises of a liberated independent state of Macedonia, created an instant army. Many members were leftover partisans from the war, who had gallantly fought against the Germans and Italians, but the majority were Slavic Macedonians who were fighting for the noble purpose of gaining independence from the oppressive Greek dominance.

This army took to the cause, fighting against the ruling Greek government, which was corrupt to the core, English influenced royally and with family dominated enterprise. To this day, Greece still does not recognize the minorities of Macedonia, which are Slavic and have their own language, customs and ethnic culture. In the 1930s, the Greeks changed all of the names of the people, villages, and towns forbidding their native language to be spoken, insisting that about 700,000 people never existed.

The original Macedonian names of some of the villages within a 50 kilometer radius that I remember include: Grazdeno, Orovo, Nivici, Vineni, Drobitista, Rabi, German, Luk, Pupli, Ostima, Bigla, and Lerin, which was the largest town. Now I am sure that I have unintentionally skipped a few, but none of these

Macedonian names exist any longer, and all have taken the Greek names imposed upon them. This was the main reason the people participated, to reclaim their original identity.

The fighting took place in Northern Greece (Macedonia) along the borders with Albania, Yugoslavia and Bulgaria. This location was strategic for the Partisans, as it provided easy access to supplies from neighboring countries, and when the push came, it allowed them to retreat into those countries to regroup. Vicious battles were taking place throughout the region, and the body count kept rising on both sides. But, with massive military injections of armaments from the United State, the government forces started to get the upper hand on the battlefield, so the Partisans were forced to adjust to the accommodations.

I was only eight years old at the time, but I vividly remember older people talking about abandoning our village, in order to avoid the harshness and consequences of war and protect the children. My village is Orovo, situated in the valley on the extreme northern border of Greece, and if you crossed over the hill, you would be in Albania. West of the village, there are high hills, wild brush and snakes. The north side is the productive side with many gardens and fields full of crops which helped provide the food and sustenance for the villagers, but the topography and the terrain made for challenging and demanding conditions. It required a considerable amount of blood, sweat, and tears to have a reasonable yield of crops. There was not any time to decompress. Life was very harsh, both economically and politically, right after World War II, and then there was the civil war. We were smack in the middle of the action. Orovo had about eighty homes, and if I remember correctly, about thirty-seven young people perished in the battle, from our village alone.

The situation of power changed periodically, and whichever side dominated at the time had the means to institute their will and recruit new converts to their cause. It became such a paradoxical situation when one member of a family was fighting, and another member of his family was on the other side of the conflict. My brother, Spiro, who was in his early twenties, was drafted to the regular army, and a couple of years later, my two sisters, Vasilka and Todora, were recruited into the Partisans movement, putting them on the opposite path, fighting against their own brother.

The decisions and orders were coming from invisible forces and were handed down to the local people, who did not have any education, knowledge, or talent to implement them in any reasonable and fair manner. Everybody acted on a whim, and anyone who had a grudge against anybody else, for whatever reason in the past, now was the "High Noon" to pay them back.

One day, acting on a tip that my brother Spiro was in Lerin, which is about 60 km from Orovo, mother took me there. I was 7 years old at the time, and somehow, by hitchhiking on trucks going in our direction, we reached the city and stayed in my Aunt Stephania's house (my mother's sister). The information about my brother being in Lerin turned out to be wrong, and we did not see him; however, that trip opened the doors towards an absolutely unseen and unheard of new world for me.

Living in Orovo, in primitive barely existing conditions, our minds had been locked in the fog of ignorance, believing that the world ended at the furthest point that the horse could take you, or just beyond the hills that surrounded the area. Now, going to Lerin, I saw cars, motorcycles, bicycles, tall buildings, stores filled with goods, masses of people for the first time, and it was totally overwhelming. Seeing homes lit by some invisible power-bulb hanging from the ceiling that was turned on and off by a switch on the wall, was total magic. I started playing with the switch on the wall, and my uncle asked me to stop. Pointing toward the bulb, I asked him what it was for, and he replied "collecting the flies". My uncle was annoyed by my stupid question, and did not comprehend my bewilderment with my new discovery.

When we returned home, I spent hours telling my friends about the things I saw, and not to being able to explain what it was exactly. Life in the village, and in the surrounding area, did not have any promising outcomes. If you were lucky, you would finish grammar school, and you would learn how to read and write, but there was no prospect of going to high school or any place higher, because there wasn't any further education available.

You are born. You grow up and work on the family fields. You learn survival instincts imposed on you by the geopolitical circumstances. You get married through prearranged agreements by your family. You have your own children, and the cycle of life starts all over again. Aha, then you die. Considering the fact that you are very lucky to reach old age, tiptoeing through the minefield, full of sickness, regional political skirmishes and wars. Welcome to the Balkans.

In France, they have a "Macedonian salad" on their menus. If you asked what that was, you were told it is "a mixture of all things." Political ambitions, nationalities, tendencies, hate, brutality, religious conflicts, jealousy, and greed were all components of daily life. Many people, including my father and grandfather, opted to leave the country and go overseas, mainly to America, Canada and Australia. They would work hard for a few years, come home with some modest savings, fix the house, buy some property or livestock, make some babies, and then leave the family again to go back to make some more money. Many single men would leave the village, and sometime later would receive a letter from the family that they were now married to someone, sight unseen. The men would assure the man that the bride was from a good family, and they have so many sheep and cows. And though those marriages lasted life times, and a joke was that was why you could not find any divorce lawyers in the vicinity of hundreds of villages.

In the fall of 1938, a group of men from the neighboring villages, including my father, Alexander, organized and decided to live in "Czuzdina." To the unknowing, it was described, but all knew that they were headed towards America. When my father left, my mother was five or six months pregnant with me, and I was born on April 28, 1939. World War II had started, and that is where this story begins.

The civil war in Greece lost the momentum of intensity; the Partisans were beaten on many fronts and started looking at various solutions to disengage themselves from the trap they had set. So their plan was to evacuate all of the children to other countries, in the name of "humanitarian action," in order to avoid the war atrocities, all the while committing the same atrocities, by snatching them from their families and submitting them to the unknown future in the foreign countries which were more devastated by the Nazis than Greece. After they moved the children, they then started transporting the Partisans all the way to Uzbekistan, an unknown, unheard of Muslim country, under the benevolence of comrade Stalin's Russia. Then came the remaining older people, who traveled through Albania, and wound up in Poland.

The evacuation of children started late March of 1948 in our area. After some quick preparations, they divided us into groups, and each group had one assigned person who was in charge and responsible for the well-being of the children. The afternoon that I was evacuated—I do not remember what day it was— we all arrived at the destination point in our village, and in the midst of indescribable conditions of the moms hugging, crying, screaming, wailing, pushing, we started to travel down the road toward the Lake Prespa.

To us kids, it was sort of an adventure, not realizing where they were taking us, and we were oblivious to the situation. But our parents were

10

bearing the brunt of what was happening to their children snatched from their arms and sent off into the unknown. Where are they going? When they are coming back? Are they going to remember us? What if something happened to us, who would take care of them when they come back? Those were questions, and there weren't any answers, but lots of speculation.

But the unthinkable element in any parents' heart was the tremendous anguish and incalculable guilt of letting their children go. If you decided to keep them home and the child is killed in the next bombing, you will be a person crucified in life-long guilt and the condemnation of your peers. But if you send the children away, not resenting the fact that the planners of the children's exodus had done some favorable propaganda, the children will go to the communist countries and be taken care of, be educated and live in peace.

So there you have it, what else do you want? Actually, nobody wanted anything else except to be left alone. But it was too late for that; too much blood had been spilled; too many young people had made the supreme sacrifice for false hopes; too many children became orphans; and too many personal tragedies took place, impacting the psyche of people for many, many years ahead.

The exodus of children was estimated to be anywhere between 27, 000 and 32,000. As we started separating from the families and strolling down to the lake, we were boarded onto some decrepit row boat and started going toward the Yugoslavian coast by passing by the village of Nivici, in which my mother was born and many relatives lived. We landed on the Yugoslavian shore, and after doing roll call to confirm that everybody was present and grouped according to our assigned units, we started marching (over rocks and prickly weeds) towards God knows where. After marching all night paired up in rows, with little kids screaming for their mothers, hungry, and physically exhausted, many of us bleeding, we finally reached the huge village of Ljubojno, Yugoslavia.

At that time, Yugoslavia was a blended country with several nationalities, languages and religions, under heavy control by Marshall Tito (who had greatly contributed to World War II). At the time, it was a country totally exhausted after two World War victories over Germany, but was now at a crossroads leaning toward political and economic stability. Having a heavily depleted economy without any industrial output of substance to begin with, and politically spurned by the USSR, it was in very precarious position. So, under these conditions, we were in Yugoslavia.

In Ljubojno, they spread us out into various rooms in schools and other buildings, in order to get some sleep. The next day, after the horrendous march the previous day and night, we awoke in the unknown country. No it was not a bad dream, it was real and we did not have a clue when it would end. We started licking our wounds, looking and crying for our mothers. The smaller children were inconsolable— hungry and screaming—and the poor ladies in charge were at the end of their wits, because there was nothing they could do except to hold and try to console the young ones. There was no food, no sanitary facilities, no beds to rest, and we were wandering around aimlessly just waiting for something to happen. But somebody was looking out for us after all, and after what felt like an eternity to us, people started serving hot soup and bread from huge vats.

We stayed in Ljubojno for three or four days under these conditions, and then they trucked us to bigger city, Bitola, and then by train to a godforsaken, primitive place, Brailovo. That is when things went from bad to worse. Hundreds of children were moved into barns and other shelters, with 20-30-40 kids per room sleeping on the floors, crying, calling for their mothers. Their noses were dripping and eyes red from crying, and the floor was full with feces. We were all scratching our heads, because by then we were full of lice. In the morning for breakfast, we each got a plate of hot water with one or two strings of macaroni—you would be extremely lucky if you got three strings. The afternoons were the same: hot water with two or three beans, and if you were not paying attention, the older boys will snatch the beans right off of your plate. That human hell lasted about seven to ten days—I can't remember exactly—before a train finally arrived at the place.

When the train arrived, they opened up a bunch of crates full of solid chunks of marmalade, and they let us eat it all. We were shoving the marmalade in our mouths with both hands, and before you swallowed the first piece, two others handfuls entered the mouth. Our cheeks were full and popping out, and there was marmalade dripping all over our faces, noses, eyes, and clothes. But who cared? We continued to shove the chunk of marmalade into our mouths before we could even swallow the previous. Then, the gluttony ended and somehow order prevailed.

We were lined up by villages, and started boarding the train. Our village, Orovo, and Grazdeno boarded the first wagon, next to the locomotive. Needless to say, after going through such a traumatic experience, having a belly full of marmalade and being on a monster of a train, for a few minutes we forget about the hell that we had crossed up to that time. After a few huffs and puffs, the train stared going off into the unknown, and our instincts were telling us that no matter where this train was taking us, it could not be as bad as what we experienced so far.

After a few hours of travel, the train stopped in the city of Nish for a few minutes, leaving us cooped up in those old, dilapidated cars. The marmalade high started to wear off and our stomachs began to growl from hunger, but nothing was forthcoming. No food and no information about what nation we were in, where are we going, why and with whom. Those were totally invisible to us. Everything was carried on in some subliminal way, and the operation was proceeding according to somebody's plans, but the operators were nowhere to be found. The older children were whispering that the Greek communist party was in charge and the other communist countries were also involved in operations. There were other points of entering of refugees, but we were totally oblivious of their fate and conditions, and some may have experienced some worse situations than us.

After a few hours of travel, the train crossed the Yugoslavian boarder and we entered Romania, and after some waiting, the train started rolling again. I am using "generic" descriptions of the time, day, people, etc, because we were so primitive and did not know the days, hours, and calendar, as we were totally illiterate, and overwhelmed by the evolving conditions. But then we reached Hungary, and immediately things started happening. First they fed us, gave us bread with marmalade (yes, marmalade again), and milk. Ah, it was the first time I had milk since we had left home. Milk and varieties of cheeses were the staples of our diet, but Yugoslavia had not yet discovered milk at that point? They had, but everything was done so secretly that people were not aware of the circumstances.

Then, they pulled us out of the cars and started fumigating the whole train. Several hoses stretched at various points of the train were spewing foggy substances inside the train. You could see steam dripping all over. Before we re-boarded the train, one by one, the Hungarian officials sprayed us with some portable gadget. We were instructed to close our eyes, and upon doing, so they pushed the lever and fog would cover us for a few seconds and then clear. After they were done, we re-boarded the train but could smell all over, whatever was applied.

The train started rolling again, but the older kids noted that the train, after each stop, was getting shorter and shorter with fewer and fewer cars. After an all-night ride, the next morning we found ourselves in yet another new country: "Welcome to Czechoslovakia!" It was a name that we had never

16

heard of before and difficult to pronounce, and it made me wonder just how many countries are there anyway? We had landed in the Moravian part of the country, in the small town of Bludov.

So there we were, in Bludov. For how long, where we were going next, nobody knew. But by turn of event, we more or less surmised that this place is going to be our anchor for some time. Everything was organized and run like a military operation. As soon as we left the train, they took us into huge barracks, and there, barbers applied their trade, cutting our hair down to the skin, stripped our clothes off of our bodies, and immediately pushing us into a huge steaming showers.

At this point, girls went to the left, boys to the right in separate wings of the building. There were people inside helping with soaps, maneuvering the shower controllers, and because what was happening was new to us, we were galloping around, avoiding the showers out of fear, because nobody was above pouring water on us. How did the water get so high and spilling on us? I am telling you – it was a real miracle. Miracle or not, after a while we grew to like it, and the officials had a difficult time kicking us out of the showers.

As soon as we got to the next room, they dressed us in uniforms— gray sweats—and then they took us to the huge dining area, where we were fed with all kinds of mostly unknown edibles. We ate as much as we wanted, which somehow in turn calibrated our metabolism, because it had been a long, long time since we had eaten a full meal. However, a different dilemma popped up on the horizon: how are we supposed to recognize each other, since they cut our hair and dressed us in the same type of sweats? The boys and girls all looked alike. Refreshed and fed, we collapsed on the mattresses, and the next morning we were under organized circumstances.

Meanwhile, many children could not find their brothers, sisters, or other relatives. Apprehension set inside their souls, and they started crying. Fears of kidnapping took over, and worse thoughts. Soon the Czech authorities saw the problems, and they immediately started communication with those invisible people who were running the whole operation. They explained what had transpired when every time we entered a country, and a few wagons were detached from the train. Usually, the last wagons, and those children traveling inside, were staged in that country. So, some children stayed in Yugoslavia, Romania, Hungary, and the remaining wagons came to Czechoslovakia. If one brother or sister was in a different wagon, and the wagon was uncoupled, then one kid found himself in Hungary, while the other in found themselves in Czechoslovakia. So what difference it makes, they were all part of the

Communist system, and we were all going to be happy and safe. At least that was the reasoning of the officials who organized the massive tragic, ill-conceived refugee plan that was undertaken.

Meanwhile, nobody had thought to recognize and react to the agony, hardship, and hell that our families felt and were going through after their children were taken for some misunderstood, far-fetched, communist, mentally flawed utopia. So on our first morning in Bludov, after the apprehension had settled, we were served breakfast in the cafeteria. Then, there was some official welcoming by various officials in the Czech language—our new home—detailing the activities for the day. It was all "Czech" to us, and we received very warm and friendly welcomes and hugging from the Czech populace.

We then hit the playground outside, investigating the place, mingling with the mass of children from other parts of Greece. All of us were somehow bewildered by all of the new surroundings and the warmth of Czech people. There was plenty of space to play and walk, but the entire perimeter of the base was fenced in, so you could not leave. But even if you could leave, where would you go? So the Czech people would come to the fence outside, and they would wave to us and we would run to them. They would touch our hands and faces, ask our names, smile with us, and give us assorted gifts, cookies, pencils, crayons, combs. We had to wait a long time to use those combs, because our heads were bald.

People were showing genuine warmth and interest toward us, which was the first time that we had experienced such direct contact with people since we left home, and the mystery was somehow slightly open about our fate and we felt somehow more secure. Within a few days, it was obvious to me that the Czechs were highly cultured and polite, and the country was very much industrialized and developed. The evidence was all around, be it the cars, bicycles, buildings or hygiene.

Up until then, everything was handled in a forced, militaristic manner, like a cattle run. We were medically examined by doctors, and we started every morning by exercising and then received lectures in general about the whole situation, and the battlefields back home. They began the preparation of placing us in various children's homes. All of the sudden, Greek functionaries arrived on the scene. They took more or less of a commanding role, implemented by Czech representatives.

It was late April 1948, and we started departing Bludov to various destinations in much smaller numbers, with two or three villages paired together. Those from Orovo and Grazdeno landed in a spectacular place called Lesna. Although we were only there for the summer, what a summer it was! The building was a huge, elegant summer home that belonged to somebody, but we could not care less about whose home it was, now it belonged to us. It was surrounded by meadows; trails, hills and valleys, and a spectacular forest of pine trees all planted in rows. At the front of the building was a huge swimming pool, about 4 feet deep and made of cement. We had a glorious summer learning how to swim, going hiking and listen to this: we would load the leftover food in barrels, put them on small wagons, and ride them downhill where there was some shelter, and we would feed the deer. We were literally bringing our hand to their mouths. For us kids, it did not get any better than touching and feeding deer, because at home, we had bears and wolves, not deer!

But, an unexpected malady spoiled our idyllic summer. A few of us, including me, contracted a goiter—whatever that is—and they had to put us in an isolated wing of the building for a week. Aha, and the food was somehow different, but we had to eat that no matter what. In Bludov, it was more of institutional bulk turned generic. Here, it was elegantly served, small portions of "Kledniky, veprovina and zely" You figure it out, what it was.

The summer eventually came to an end, and we were transported from Lesna to a small town called Sobotin, where I spent a considerable amount of time. Goodbye Lesna, which to this day, I remember and dream about as being the best spent time of my youth. Welcome to Sobotin! Sobotin was a spread out, mountainous, large village or small town (I don't know which), that is locked within a bigger city, Sumperk. I don't think anything ever happened in Sobotin, except that it was the home of the factory, which made the well-known bicycles, Velamous.

Our arrival shook the town out of its perpetual, easy-going way of life. A few hundred, wild, unrestrained children, even when on their best behavior, will create a big commotion and impact— and who said we were well behaved? As a matter of fact, who said that we behaved at all? I don't remember under which criteria we were split among four buildings; however, we found ourselves mixed up with many unknown kids from other parts of Greece. Many of them spoke with some strange dialects that we had never heard before, and vice versa. But time mellows everything, and atones for our transgressions. Divided by age, we started going to classes and learning how to speak the Czech language, as well the basics of many other subjects.

And what happened to the promises to our families back home that we were leaving on a temporary basis to avoid being killed by government soldiers? What is going on? Our families, are they alive? Nobody was talking about that subject. The Czechs were taking good care of us and gradually we blended with the circumstances. Building #6 was the administrative headquarters, the central kitchen for all others buildings, where they cook the meals and trucked them to the smaller kitchens at each building. Buildings #5-4-3 and 2 were our living quarters. I don't know what happened to Building #1 because it did not exist.

We had very hectic schedule every day, taking accelerated classes to catch up our stupid heads with our ages and therefore, we were discovering new worlds in knowledge and amassing new facts about our planet. We learned that the planet is round. Some bigger boys (with dense brains) did not accept the theory; according to them, it was a story to scare us in order to keep us together because if you escape, you will reach the point where you will fall off the planet.

One day they took us to the movies. As it was our first time, we were full of apprehension, everything was new to us. The movie was a nature type. It started with music blaring, some small creek full with geese, and a train approaching from far, far away. As the train came closer and closer, the locomotive was puffing steam, getting bigger and bigger and it seemed to be coming toward us, filling the screen completely. Screams erupted, chairs fell to the floor, pandemonium broke out and the movie stopped. The lights came on, and half the crowd, including me, were under the chairs, avoiding the locomotive which we thought had just jumped the track. It scared the living crap out of us. That was the first and last movie we saw for a long time.

The older kids had a field day, mocking us, and laughing at us. But life continued. I started making friends with the other kids and after some time, they provided us with Macedonian language classes, in the afternoons. The Greek kids were taught Greek, the Macedonians-Macedonian, and the day classes were strictly in Czech. And living all together, the Greeks learned Macedonian fluently, us Macedonians learned Greek, so at same time we were learning two other languages without effort.

As the time progressed, we adapted quite well in Sobotin, knew all the ins and outs of the area, knew the best fruit trees and gardens and on many, many occasions, unfortunately, we were helping ourselves like we were entitled to the fruits of the local owners, which became a point of contention after a while.

Within the interior of our psyche, there was a trait, which somehow, compelled us to do some silly or downright stupid things which either we could not comprehend and or we were showing remnants which were imbedded into our genes due to the fact of conditions and nature, where we were born.

But raiding the orchards and gardens and other pranks continued for some time. In the summer, while the school was out, we used to go on various field trips. One summer, we went to Prague an old, historic city, full with church spires, and magnificent castles. History seemed to be dripping down the walls. We saw it all, and we were awed by the buildings. But, somehow, we found a way for mischief. We went to the Prague Zoo one hot summer day and saw families with young kids licking ice cream cones. We were penniless, just looking at them and salivating. Then we went to a cheese factory. At that time, it was fact among us that you had to possess a pocketknife. If you did not have a pocketknife, you were out of the clique. Every tree within our reach was carved with our names on it. The Czechs used to say: "Jmena hloupych na vsech sloupich", but it did not bother us.

Going back to the cheese factory, we put those pocket knives to very good use. We would pick up the loaves of cheese and cut a big chunk from the bottom and put it back. When we boarded the bus to get back to the dorms we stayed at, we had more than enough cheese to open a store.

The next day, they took us to an ice cream parlor. It was a long building with serving window in the middle. The guide said "come on kids, form a line along the building, and everybody will get a cone". And so we did. For the first time in our life, we tried ice cream and it sure tasted great. We would get a cone, go to the end of the building and turn around and get back in the line. By the third round, the sales ladies began screaming at our guide! "You told me there were 47 kids and I already served over 80?" That was the end of our ice cream run.

The next day we visited the largest store in Prague. Our heads were turning so fast, we were getting whiplash, looking at clothes, toys, shoes, so much of everything. And then we saw a display of trains on several tables. Like a natural landscape, buildings, hills, waterfalls, and train stations. One train goes left, the other right, then they bypass each other. The rails went up, the lights went on and that exhibition left us numb and speechless. But no matter what we did, we did not forget to apply our skills. Again in the bus, every brave soul started pulling from our pockets, different types and sizes of the wagons we managed to take from the display. The only thing we did not take was the locomotive.

We were attending two schools, depending on which dorm you lived in. I was at dorm 4 and going to the smaller school, north of town. It was about 2 or more miles away, and every school day you had to walk to school, no buses at all. In good weather, we managed quite well, walking in rows, under supervision, but come winter, it was a different kind of animal. The winters were brutal, with wind, cold temperatures. By the time we reached the school, we were frozen, red faces, noses dripping with stuff, clothes full of cold snow and ice. And our feet were numb from the cold.

But the Czech kids didn't have it any better either. We were fed much better than the local kids and I very often shared my lunch with them. The principal of the school was a weird and unkempt fellow. His name was Mr. Kurtz, and he was a very strong disciplinarian. God-forbid if you had to go to his office for any minor infraction of the rules. He would grab and pull your hair or the top of your ears and extract a promise that you would not be sent back to him. And promise or not, I don't think his method worked very well, because I was one of his frequent clients.

One day Mr. Kurtz comes out of his office into the hallway, carrying huge glass framed portrait of President Gottwald. He searched for a spot on the wall, picked a spot that already had a nail, and ordered me to bring him a chair so he could reach the nail. I hurried and put the chair under the spot. The Principal climbed on the chair with the portrait, lunged forward and hung the portrait (or so he thought). And then within half a second, bang, the portrait lies on the floor, shattered in pieces. What happened? What happened is that the nail he saw on the wall was not a nail, it was a fly. When I was bringing him the chair, I was praying the fly will be still be there and it was.

"Nowadays you can't trust anybody", the principal murmured under his breath, and asked me to clean the mess. Between feeling sorry for him and trying not to burst out laughing, I cleaned the mess, but then I exploded into laughter. And when my friends asked what was so funny, I told them but I said that I was the culprit who misjudged the nail and the fly because I genuinely felt sorry for him. After a few weeks, Mr. Kurtz disappeared and one of the teachers mentioned that he was discharged for some inappropriateness. I did not realize that you could lose your job for dropping the portrait of the President. Besides, it was the stupid fly's fault, not his.

Going to school, actually, we had two options to walk. One through town was shorter and better protected from the winter elements and most of the other times. But above was a paved road for the car traffic, longer to school, but much better view of the town sitting in the valley. On the side of the road was an immobilized German tank remaining from the World War II. We used to mount the tank, enter the cabin, hang over the body and turret and pretend. If you cut through the private field downward, you will hit the town road and you were very close to the school, eliminating some distance, making a loop from the traffic road. In one of these trips, we noticed an apple tree loaded with fruit, smack in the middle of the field.

So we put that fact in a to-do list when the harvest time came. In the fall of 1950, one late afternoon, going home from school, we put our plan in action. There were six guys. The plan was that three of us would climb the apple tree and the other three will collect the apples we would throw to them and, at home, we would split the bonanza. I climbed on top of the branches, with two guys below me and started throwing the apples. All of the sudden, the ground guys started running toward the tank, the lower guys jumped down and managed to escape a lady with a dog, coming from the house. I was still on top of the apple tree, but she did not look up, and when she left, I jumped down collected the apples and I was gone.

By the fall of 1950, they moved me to dorm #3 and I started attending the bigger school, much brighter and closer to the dorm. We had some terrific teachers: Miss Hajkova, older than the rest, a science teacher and first rate person. She had a warm personality and was dedicated to the utmost. The tougher it was, the easier she made it. Ms. Praizova taught Czech and Geography. She was tall and skinny, looking undernourished, with too much rouge on her face. Wait, what? I was a young lad 9-10 years old, what do I know about makeup? Well then, I did not know anything, but I remember these things so vividly that I can describe them completely in the present time. Ms. Kolarova was hard working and on the proletarian side. I think if she would be in the present time in the USA, she would have a high position in the teachers union. And Mr. Vladimir. The pupil's teacher; soccer, hockey, sports; go and see Mr. Vladimir.

Now the year is 1950, the civil war in Greece ended in 1949, with the total defeat of the partisans, the government returned with superior armaments and planes by the USA (the Truman Doctrine) pulverized the fighting field.....but what happened to our people? My Mother and sister-in-law, Pana, were in the village and don't forget the grandmother. Brother Spiro was in the army and sisters Vasilka and Todora with the partisans. And we don't have any contact whatsoever. Maybe we can return home, there is no fighting anymore, and not all children left the country so there must be some life, some continuity so we can return. Not so fast. Sometime in the summer of 1951, I received some strange letter addressed directly to me!

It was mailed from Poland, written in the Latin alphabet, the envelope that is. It was a letter written in Macedonian and I immediately recognized the writing. It was a letter from my mother. I was flabbergasted but why from Poland? My mother was one of the very few people of her generation that could write and read. I read the letter again and again and still could not comprehend it. It tells me that by the end of the fighting, the same scumballs who evicted us, organized a massive withdrawal of the civilian population from many borderline villages. They were taken through Albania by boats and were settled in Poland. My Mother, my sister-in-law and grandmother were together in the town of Zgorzelec, with many other people from our village. But, my mother did not know where my sisters or brother are. So that much of the promises the communists were telling us. We will never return back to our motherland.

A few months later, I received another mysterious envelope, this time from Tashkent, Uzbekistan USSR. This letter was from my sister, Vasilka, who after the defeat was transported with Sister Todora and many other partisans who were lucky to survive the slaughter, to the end of the world, Muslim country Uzbekistan. All these accommodations to contact the families, were carried by the Red Cross and sooner or later, either the Red Cross or our families were making periodic contacts with us. The correspondence started flowing between the family. Mother informed me that my brother was discharged from the army and was in Lenn and the village was in the total ruins from the fighting and it became a ghost town; nobody was left there.

In 1951, my brother left Greece for Canada and settled in Toronto. Now bear with me: Once we were a total family in our village, we had houses, livestock, farms, gardens, relatives, friends, the total package. Then we were swayed by the communists, who told us that whatever we have, is nothing to compare to what we are going to have, if only Greece would become a communist state, under Russian influence. In order to achieve this, we would have to start a civil war, where thousands and thousands of young people would lose their lives and many others were maimed and scarred for life! And now you go and find the guilty. The guilty are in Moscow. General Markos, Communist Chief Zachariadis and all of their henchmen hid as war criminals traitors in Moscow and you never heard of them again. Meantime, our families stand as follows:

I am in Czechoslovakia
Mother is in Poland
Father is in USA
Brother is in Canada
Sisters are in USSR

Next brother (Spiro) is married and has 3 daughters. He is in Canada. His wife Pana, is in Poland with the youngest daughter Kristina, the middle daughter Mary, and the older daughter, Teresa, are in Czechoslovakia. My younger sister, Todora, was single, but my older sister, Vasilka was married and had a son, Michael. Her husband, Alex, was in Greece. Their son Michael was in Czechoslovakia and sister was in Uzbekistan. Now, tuck your blankets snugly and try to sleep peacefully. Can you do it? If you could, you have a stone where your heart should be. So the lessons of the liberation war: inept, uneducated zealots, with the tails under their asses, hobbled to different countries but the elite, the higher echelon, the hardened communists landed in Moscow.

The chief of the Greek Communist Party, Zachariadis, stayed in Moscow, until his death. The grotesque General Markos, after many years in Moscow, was permitted to return back to Greece, with all the perks. His Greek citizenship was restored and he was given a pension! And he lived comfortable life until his death. In our Macedonian language, when a person dies, we say that the person "umre", but for the animals, when they die, we use a different word, "psoisa", which infers the same fate, but different genre. So, on my own, to show total disrespect and utmost outrage for what they did to many thousands of people, I declare that they did not die humanely, but they "psoisa" like dogs, which they were.

Meantime, in Czechoslovakia the psychological pressure is around us. It started soon after we got situated, first slowly and gradually more intensely, as the time went by and it reached the culmination point. It was the pro-Russian propaganda, which they try on a daily basis to embed in our conscience. The virtues of Communism, the Russian superiority in every aspect of life, the Russian leaders were worshipped, Stalin was a super-human. We were taught Russian songs and the Russian language became compulsory in all grades.

The Czech technology was far superior than Russian, but every item was "discovered" by Russians first. When the Russian army liberated Czechoslovakia from the Germans, many soldiers were giving their horses in exchange for a bicycle, which many of them saw for the very first time in their life. They will take the clock from the wall and demand that the watchmaker make him 5 wristwatches. Those were the tales the Czechs were telling us.

And in the sport of hockey, where the Czech were second to the Canadians, the Russian did not have even one ice rink. The Czech supplied them with the equipment and coaches to teach them the game, and after that they became adequate at it, it was dwelled on us, the Russian workers invented the hockey game in Siberia, after they crossed the lake to move around during the winters. All these facts, we learned from the Czech teachers and ordinary people dealt with every day. The Czechs hated the whole propaganda and lies, but the communist party members, seeing the personal benefits to themselves, prescribed the utopia and lived by it.

And so did we as young children at impressionable ages. It was very easy to believe because the Russian army defeated the all-powerful Germans didn't they? All by themselves to boot. At least that's how we were taught. They paraded us in many events, with the Czech and Russian flags waving, the loudspeakers were blasting on full decibel meter, introducing us to the crowds, with the lame worn out platitudes: The heroic children from Greece who valiantly rejected the oppressive life in Greece, under the dominancy of American imperialism. On the other hand, from the point of being taken care in every aspect of life, we were in the best hands. We were taught discipline, personal behavior, respect for all, toughness, self-sustenance and on top of all that, received an excellent education.

Every summer, when the school was out, we were visiting various parks, castles, underground caves, and many other places. As soon as the school year ended, they will send us to the barber and the girls would have their hair trimmed, but us boys, were shaved to the core. Three of us refused to have our heads shaved and they left us alone, however, many other kids started complaining. About a week later, we woke up in horror, overnight somebody came in and ran clippers right down the middle of our heads leaving a shaved path from the front to the back. Obviously, we were the laughing stock of everybody for a week, because they would not cut the rest of our hair as a form of punishment. So that is what I meant about being taught discipline.

On the edge of the town there was a huge swimming hole/pool and we were doing lots of swimming every summer. Between the pool and railroad tracks were some concrete slabs and we used to lie on top of the slabs and dry out and suntan. Somebody started, and we all picked up the habit that as soon we saw the train coming from Sumperk, we would disrobe and lay naked on top of the slabs. The passengers were all gawking at us. It was a stupid thing, but it felt good at the time. So the school year 1950 started, new dorms, new teachers, new friends and the life was good. Mr. Vladimir introduced us to sporting events; track & field, skiing, and hockey. But we could not afford to buy any equipment and used to borrow or steal different sport apparatus, so sometimes one ski was longer that the other, one skate good, the other tightened to the shoe with strings, but we kept going regardless.

Then started soccer, volleyball, and I found myself hooked on sports for life. The early fifties were the golden times for the Czech athletics, especially in track and field events. Their hero, Emil Zatopak and his wife Dana, were collecting Olympic gold medals and were known all around the world. And Emil Zatopak became my personal hero and I became an avid participant in track and field. I started a scrapbook with all the records, events and pictures. For many years, I was a sort of walking encyclopedia for all records. And then came the darn Russians breaking the records every week in all categories until they mixed me up completely. My computer "blew a chip".

In the dorm, in a very peculiar way, I met a fellow from a different village back home. Skinny, rusty hair and full of freckles on his face. Efto was his name. Every day during the dinner hour he would walk to the girls table and would demand the meat from their dishes. Many were intimidated and gave it to him. He would spit into the dish if they refused and they would go hungry. One evening, he did it to a girl sitting next to me. We were sitting on a long bench-style tables. The girl started crying and got up and left.

There was no make-up kitchen. If you miss your mealtime, you wait until next meal, which for her meant until next day. "Efto, come here", I hollered at him and he came. You forgot something, I said to him. What? I grabbed the girls dish with the spit and shoved the whole thing in his face. You forgot your spit, and that's what. The rest started laughing at him. The food started dripping over his face and that was the last time Efto spit in anyone's dish. For a couple of weeks, we were growling at each other like dogs, but I was much bigger than him and was confident that if it came to a physical altercation, I would clean his clock. And as fate would have it, a few weeks later, I had to clean him anyhow. It was raining the whole week. All the rooms in the dorms had very high ceilings and all light fixtures were globes hanging down on a pipe. So Efto went to use the bathroom and somehow the globe from all that rain was full with water, broke loose and hit him smack in the head. Here runs Efto from the bathroom, screaming, all wet, and bleeding from the head and face, with his pants down, falling on the floor. I grab a towel, run to him, wiped him down, pick up his pants and took him to the nurse's office. From then on, we became the best friends!

A big part of our communal life was our annual contribution toward our wellbeing. Seasonally, we were working in smaller or larger groups toward securing the resources of various commodities. During the harvest season, we would pick up potatoes by the truck loads, and then store them in storage bins or dig up a huge hole and cover them with hay and dirt. The trucks will dump mountains of coal and we would shovel it through the windows, down into the basement of the huge storage building. We would go and harvest carrots, green beans, and very often, hops for the beer-making industry. They would show us certain vegetation and we would go to the woods to collect them for pharmaceutical use. We would plant thousands and thousands of tree seedlings and that activity, I just hated! No gloves, you dig the opening, put the seedling in and step on it to secure it and all day keep repeating the same moves until my hands will blister.

Somehow the truck with food would always come late. The forest was always full of stupid garden snakes and we would catch them and scare the hell of the girls. But what I liked was that we will go to the forest where hundreds of trees were already cut and lying on the ground and will trim the branches with small axes. Then we will erect tents and sleep over in the woods and next day continue trimming until all trees were done. And they will bring the trees to the dorm and cut them to the size about 1½ feet. And the best part – we will split them in pieces and stack them.

The supervisors in charge of the labor related activities would compel us to take care of our buildings, some outside general cleaning, mend some fences and fix up some broken doors, screens, etc. Which in first place, we were the guilty party who broke them. In the cafeteria, during the breakfast, the supervisor would announce that he needs 4-5 strong boys, and before he finished the word "strong", our hands were in the air so we can impress the girls. But then he would finish the sentence, "but stupid" with strong emphasis on the word "stupid", and a few of us got stuck with our hands up confirming who was stupid; everyone would laugh. But sometimes raising your hand was liberating us to skip the school and the others would resent it.

And the time would progress and we would learn and grow, and march, and be indoctrinated in the communist dogma; how the workers in the USA always go on strikes, being abused by factory bosses, and the blacks were denied of all the opportunities and abused and discriminated against and yet, we would see American films where blacks mingled with the whites, going shopping, to the restaurants, dancing and on the way to collect the unemployment check, driving such a huge car, where here you could hardly navigate some narrow streets.

Yes, I know that life was not a panacea here either, and the movies distract the reality of life, but there, we as children, of a political abortion, caused by the communists, we were taken care of, but the average worker could not afford to buy a suit. You could buy the pants and by the time you save for the coat, the pants were already worn out. And shortages of food and other commodities prevailed throughout the country on consistent basis and even if you had some money, the goods were not available.

Academically and athletically, I excelled, and that fact gave me many chances to go and represent my school at many competitions outside Sobotkin, but the mischief was still in us. When we were taught about conductivity of electricity, the teacher, Ms. Hajkova, was warning us not to touch any loose wiring and not to touch any person with live wire. The teacher explained that if ten people held hands and the first touches live wire, all ten are going to feel the electric shock. Miss Hajkova was asking us, "Do you understand that?" and of all the students, only Vangel Sivakov, a lovely goofball raises his hand. "I would like to know, Vangel asks, if the first person holding the live wire, and we screw a bulb in the last person's rear will the bulb light?" We were all absolutely astonished with the question, but when the teacher erupted laughing, so did we and the teacher explained, "Vangel, the bulb will light only if you are the last guy in line."

We started the school year of 1952, and I was in the seventh grade. The spring of 1953 will be the fifth year since we left homeland. One morning in March 1953, our normal routine was interrupted. The radio, through all the speakers in the building, was playing mourning marches, which was the usual procedure when some big politico had died. But this morning was unusually tense, you could feel the tension in the air. When we sat for breakfast the supervisor came in and explained the very sad news that the great leader of all the peace-loving people in the world, Generalissimo Stalin died. The supervisor was still talking, but nobody was paying attention. Pandemonium broke out, all of the girls started crying, the servants were all wiping their eyes, everyone was stunned and nobody knew what to do or how to behave. When the news broke all over, the whole country was glued to their radios listening to all commentaries from around the world. And the preparations were showing on the news reels in the movies. And in detail described on the radio for the masses. The dignitaries were gathering in Moscow, and obviously President Klement Gottwald represented Czechoslovakia and he had a full entourage with him.

Upon returning from Moscow, the president apparently caught a cold and was not feeling well and a short time later, also died. It was a double whammy of bad news for the ruling party and a period of mourning until the situation settled. Everything was done quietly, on outside with as little news as possible, but within the ranks of the party a big blood-letting was happening and the victor and new President of the Republic was Antonin Zapotovsky. The King is dead, long live the King. For us, however, the situation was constant.

The current problem we had was an "invasion of the frogs." Between dorms 3 and 4, there was a huge pond which was frozen in the wintertime and where we conducted intensive skating and hockey playing. Even without proper equipment or gloves, we would skate and play all during our free time, with our faces red and our noses dripping with mucous. And it was the greatest feeling. But come summer, the pond became infested with thousands of frogs and they would never stop croaking, keeping us awake at nights. And after a "strategic meeting" we came up with the sure plan of eliminating the unwanted enemy.

On the top of the hill, there was an open spot and all day we were gathering loose branches and broken trees. Then we started a huge fire and then the "Bucket Brigade" came to action. Equipped with buckets and different containers, we will swoop on the pond, fill the buckets with frogs and dump them into the fire. While we were going to refill the buckets, we had "trained specialist" on the periphery of the fire with sharpened sticks and every frog, who escaped was stabbed, and put back into the fire. We would show the stupid frogs who was the boss. The trips to the pond continued with the flames getting bigger and bigger, and huge dark plumes of smoke started coming out and stinking like hell. We did not realize that the frogs were so greasy. Then the smoke overtook the flames and started rising and going toward the town. Warning sirens started blasting and few minutes later, the firemen showed up, not being able to bring the truck up the hill.

And then the police came, and when they realized that it was not a normal game going on, all of us, about 15, wound up at the police precinct while we let the firemen take care of the fire. Later, the supervisor came and took us home. After intense lecturing, for the next month we were marked men. Not only did we have to clear the fire area, tiptoeing through the tulips, I mean frogs, but for a full month, we had to keep clean the premises in the dorm and cooperate with the sanitation department in the town and clean and sweep the public paths and parks. Our nickname was "The Frog Brigade".

One unfortunate and very sad event happened on the pond. One child somehow fell in the water and drowned. Most of my friends and I had not experienced anybody dying that close to us. Seeing the death first hand was very frightening to us and very upsetting. I remember that Mr. Kril, who was the top supervisor, carried the casket in his huge limousine and all of us were properly instructed and dressed for the sad occasion and marched to the cemetery for the burial. Mr. Kril was a distinguished educator who had a wife and one son who was our age, and was attending the same school with us. His name was Ivo and we were very good friends. They were living in one run-down house in the town, with bricks missing on outside, but very neat on the inside. A few of us were going to help

Mr. Kril on regular basis until the house was fixed and landscaped.

The family was not local. Mr. Kril was brought from some big city and that's the reason he stayed in the old house. Mrs. Kril was very refined lady, always smiling and always baking and cooking for us. Mr. Kril always offered us money, but we never accepted it (even the juvenile trouble makers had a code of ethics) but we settled on Ivo teaching us how to ride the bike.

The summer of 1953 was gone and the school year started. I was attending the 8th grade. In the late winter of 1954 Ms. Hajkova called me out of the class, to the office. "What family do you have George and where are they" she asked while taking notes. When we finished all she said was one word, "Skoda" which meant "too bad." I started thinking what was that all about but nobody afterward approached me or said anything and I forgot about it. In late March, some officials came and called us on the side, me and several other boys and girls. The Red Cross had started an action of unifying the families and many parents and relatives came from Poland to Czechoslovakia and many children went to Poland to their families. I don't know what criteria they used to connect the families, but with me it was my grandmother being too old to come from Poland so me and my two nieces, who were in a different city, were going to Poland. After 6 years in Czechoslovakia, where I absolutely loved it, and got used to that having so many friends, Czechs and otherwise, having plans and dreams about the future, I have to abandon that and move to a new country, start all over again, learning new language and all my dreams were left behind along with friends and teachers.

On April 1, 1954, after tears and hugs from friends
and teachers, we boarded the train and went to
Poland, to whatever was awaiting us. From the train, I
made sure to see the concrete slabs at the pool, where
we were playing, naked, and some bitter-sweet
memories crossed my mind. In a short time, we were
in Poland. We changed the train toward Zgorzelec,
where our families were waiting and the thought that
we are going to reunite with our mothers after 6 years
of separation helped soften the sad feelings of leaving
Czechoslovakia.

On April 2, 1954, we arrived in Zgorzelec. Report
for duties in Poland, but without any salutation. A
couple of soldiers held us inside the train until the
regular passengers disembarked which gave me a few
minutes to scan the crowd. A sea of people were
waiting outside, straining their necks toward the
windows, but I could not see my mother.

Obviously, the newest fashion had not arrived in
Zgorzelec because the whole scene resembled the
moment we departed from Orovo. All the women were
dressed in black dresses with various dark colors,
covering their heads. And here comes the moment: my
sister-in-law, Pana, grabs me by the hand, and mother
runs toward me and hugs me to the point that I could

not breathe. And immediately, you feel the warmth, the special aura emitting from every mother, toward these children, the kisses, the hugs, other relatives swarming around you and they hug you and ask questions, such as if I saw their sons or daughters, where they were situated in different towns and are they coming soon to Poland. Gradually, after long awaited reunions, the people started departing toward different directions of town. Mother and Aunt Ristana and few other relatives were walking in front and my nieces and their mother and other relatives were right behind us. We started walking toward home, occupying the whole road and oncoming vehicles had to maneuver around us because nobody could budge us. Every street light was a green light for us. (Was there any street light? I don't remember.)

We came home to the 4th floor of our apartment and after seeing my grandmother and hugging her, I realized that she could not see at all. She was touching me, scanning my face and my body, tears falling freely and commanding "Boy you are big". Grandma said she "begged God not take me until you return and I can see you." And then the doors never closed, people coming, visiting, and going, all distant relatives and villagers from Orovo. I did not know that many people, but it seemed the whole village came. At a free moment I mentioned to mother, "you did not tell me in your correspondence about grandmother being blind. "And what you, as a kid would have done about that. Did you not have enough problems, being alone all these years by yourself?" We celebrated until the early hours and I had not been kissed by so many people ever. The next day I had to adjust to a totally different routine since they did not keep us in Czechoslovakia a couple of months longer to finalize the school year.

Now what's next? There we were under the Czech government compulsory school and set lifestyle, here we are with our families who don't have any influence over anybody. My mind was flying all over. I was nervous. It was very unsettling feeling. I was hot and desperate to go out but where? I hardly knew anything. Then mother came and we went outside, not to disrupt the rest. And we are walking on the street and mother asks me some questions, which at that time, did not make any sense to me. And then she tells me that somebody had talked to her, when we came here, and said that we will stay until summer is over, then they are going to take us to a different city to attend school. Who mother? Who told you that? One Greek man who is a big shot at the office in the municipal building. And that is what I was waiting to hear, that I will have a chance to continue with schooling.

The idled period of time, since arriving in Poland was well served. It enabled me to sort of decompress from all the highs and lows, get used to family life again, trying to adjust to a slightly different flow of life than Czechoslovakia, start learning the Polish language, oh, and discovering the geography of the area. A couple of weeks later, another group of children arrived from Czechoslovakia and then many friends from Sobotin and we started meeting and socializing among us without the restrictions imposed on us from the communal lifestyle in Czechoslovakia. When we decided to come home, we were coming to our parents, and we had a choice of what kind of food we would eat and what we would wear next day.

My best friends, several of them, from Sobotin, came to Zgorzelec, and occasionally we would fall into juvenile behavior. During my life in Sobotin, Leon Kerazovski and Vasil Anastasovski were my best friends because from the beginning we were together except Vasil was a year older and always a grade ahead. And don't forget Vangel Sivakovski with the bulb in his ass, always shined the path at night.

My Father in the USA somehow lost due to the upheaval. When my brother came to Toronto and told him the story, we started corresponding and the whole family was in touch. Things started looking up. We were separated, but by the grace of God, we were all alive and brother and sisters, although fighting against each other, came out of that in one piece, not being wounded or harmed.

And also some strange transition took over me. I discovered that since the family did not speak the Polish language, I became the liaison for them in any need and communication. And I also found the instinct within me to care and worry about their well-being and lost many aspects of my "Devil may care" attitude and felt instantly matured for my age. When Leon came to Zgorzelec, he brought me a book I was reading but did not finish. I had returned it to one of the teachers from whom I borrowed it. She wrote beautiful remembrance note, dated it and signed it. And after 50 years later, I still have it.

Zgorzelec is a border town on the river Visla. The river divides the city into two sides, the other, Goerlitz, belonged to East Germany. The cities are connected with a massive concrete bridge and on both sides were armed guards. I never saw any sort of vehicles crossing the bridge on the Polish side. Along the Visla river was a sandy path, always maintained and patrolled by soldiers looking for footprints. And also, a tall 8 foot barbed wire fence, so if some stupid person wanted desperately to come to Poland, he or she had to cross the river, follow a plowed path and cross over a barbed wire fence to get to the street. The security guards were hiding from their own shadows.

So the summer conclusively was coming to the end and again we were recruited to go to different schools, but first we went to a city on the Baltic Sea – Szczecin. There was a huge settlement of children who originally had come to Poland from Greece. To my sadness, Leon was persuaded by his family to stay in Zgorzelec and some in-law through his aunt, was going to train him to become a shoemaker. He resented that decision all his life. In Szczecin, we blended with the "locals" for a couple of weeks and we were interviewed for what kind of schools we wanted to attend Again, with no parents and no guidance, it was difficult to make the right decisions, but my desire was always to be either a photojournalist or building engineer.

Photojournalist? Forget it. Poland was in total ruins and they needed workers, engineers and builders. So a group of us went to Wroclaw (formerly the German city of Breslaw). Our administrative base was "The Central" at Poniatowski Street, but the school and the dorms were located on the edge of the city and very easily reached by bus or street car. The name of the suburb was Psie Pole, which means "Dog Field." Before school started, we had some free time and did not have restrictions on our time nor did we report our presence to anyone. Dinner time! Are you here? Go and eat; you are not there? Fine, stay hungry. So we would climb on the street cars and most of the day we would ride through the city. A city it was not. You would see a few houses here, a few there, but most of the Wroclaw was in ruins. Whole blocks of streets were dotted with piles and piles of remnants of what used to be houses. Whoever was bombing the city, they done a hell of a good job but we remember the circumstances and, therefore, it had to be done.

But you could see new construction taking place all over the city, especially in downtown, with new train stations and high rises for new housing. At present, Wroclaw is a very dynamic, academic, medical and industrial powerhouse and plays a vital role in Polish economy. Poland had slightly different educational system. You could go to a straight high school (lyceum), or choose a school more oriented toward your future with specific curriculum (technicum). Upon graduation, you had a specific trade in mechanics, construction, planning, surveying, etc. The technical school in Psie Pole was highly rated and few of us were very happy to enroll.

So the school year started and from the beginning, we encountered some rough patches. The jargon was all technical, different calculations, angles, forces working opposite each other, measurements, strength, metallurgy, etc. and secondly, the Polish language. We were only a few months in Poland, and to get command of the language, definitely would take more time to learn it. So over the weekend, we immediately ran to our "mothership" at Poniatowski Street and complained about the situation. So Monday comes, and at school, a supervisor from the "Central" came to see what could be done, and upon seeing 3 Chinese students at the campus, his assignment became that much easier.

He huddled all 14 of us in a room and gave it to us from all barrels. You sissies, lazy guys from Czechoslovakia, what do you expect but hard work and study! Look at them, Chinese students, they don't speak any Polish, and have started from the bottom. If you are hungry, come to the Central, if you are sick, come to the Central, if you need supplies, come to the Central, but don't you ever come complaining about learning difficulties. If you need help, ask the Chinese how they cope with it. We put our tails between our legs and left totally humiliated. That was the end of learning difficulties. And those darned Chinese, all of them named Kim, had to show up at the same time when the Superintendent came? I am telling you, nothing but conspiracy.

As we were getting used to the circumstances, time also did not stand still and all of the sudden, Christmas was upon us and we had two weeks off. It was three hours ride by train to Zgorzelec and for the first time, in so many years, we celebrated a holiday with our families. Mother could not wait to see me again and many friends and relatives were visiting.

There was so much food and we had such a good time that the two weeks passed so fast, and I had to go back to school. But I got so used to being home those two weeks and felt so homesick that a thought crossed my mind to stay home. But seeing few friends aimlessly drifting around and Leon's shoemaking endeavor, fizzling, woke me up and marching I went to the train station and back to school. The school had athletic facilities, and I got involved in basketball and boxing. And in springtime, track and field, plus studies and then the first year was over.

For two weeks, we went on vacation in northern Poland, (Pojezerce Pomorskie) where there were many lakes and beautiful surroundings, and many Polish friends, who helped me very much with their language. But we had to cook for ourselves and everybody was getting daily assignments. One day, two of us had to boil the potatoes in a huge aluminum pot outside on the fire pit. When the potatoes were done, we picked the pot by the handles and walk few steps to the lake to drain the water and if you are not concentrating, accidents happen. We tipped the pot too fast and half the potatoes fell in the lake. No problem,

57

putting them back, they cooled in the water, but we were worried about the cleanliness, and did not want anybody to get sick. Aha, we took the pot in the kitchen, rinsed the potatoes with water from the sink, and everybody lived happily ever after. And after a relaxing vacation, we came back home for the rest of the summer a year older.

The initial euphoria of reuniting with the family was slightly fading. You stand looking at the situation differently. In addition to the usual family chores, Mother was also fully occupied with the care of my grandmother, who was totally incapacitated and blind. Pana, my sister-in-law, who had three girls and a job, was also over-worked and various strains of life occasionally would show their ugly head. The drive to unify families was growing and taking different directions. People started leaving Poland and going to Australia or Canada, where they had relatives. Also, a few went to USA. The Greek government started issuing return visas to women whose husbands fought on the government side and were separated. Panic set in among the people who did not qualify for this condition but nevertheless wanted to go home to their properties. The cold war was at its height. My brother started the effort to bring his family to Canada, but it was time-consuming initiative. My sister's husband found himself in USA, in Lorraine, Ohio, where his uncle had brought him. My sister was still in Tashkent and her son Mial was in Czechoslovakia.

So most of the summer I spent working on the farms, harvesting different crops and performing different jobs. A couple of Macedonian entrepreneurs had agreements to provide workers to local farmers. Every morning an uncovered wagon, towed by a tractor, would appear at a set place and you could to go to work. In the evening, the tractor would bring you back, the foreman would pay you cash for the day and the next morning, you would do the same thing all over again. No border patrol would hassle you, no OSHA poke into safety and there was no extradition (back to where?). So finally the summer was running out of time and I was going back to school. I made few bucks, bought some clothes for myself and gave the rest to Mother to spend on my Grandmother.

So one day, all fourteen of us took the train, went to the "Central", packed our school supplies, and whatever we could steal, and went back to school. This time I was genuinely looking toward the school year and the sports. The Chinese students also were there, but where they spent the summer, I don't know. We tried to communicate with them, but the Polish language was so difficult for them that they had trouble pronouncing the words. So I avoided them.

The Christmas of 1955 I spent at home and then 1956 is here. In school, the curriculum was getting more intense, we started working with different testing instruments in the metallurgical lab and as spring of 1956 was approaching, the track and field activities increased considerably. In the fifties and sixties, the Russians started dominating the sporting events, and the rest of the countries under Russian domination started investing into sports to prove to the west that their system was producing a better and healthier society, hence the emphasis on track and field. However, in my case, I got hooked up on athletics in Czechoslovakia influenced by the great Emil Zatopek. Pole vaulting, high jump, triple jump, javelin and long running were my specialties. One Saturday in April, after we finished the silly ritual at breakfast table, boarded the buses and went to the stadium where many other schools participated in the athletic meet. Aha, the silly ritual was that at breakfast table, they used to put basket full of sliced bread. So whoever came earliest would take all the bread he wanted and the guys coming later, no bread for you. So we agreed that nobody would take the bread until all guys are present. Then one of us will hit the edge of the basket, all slices will fly to the air, and we jump and grab the slices in the air. If you grab 3, they are yours, if you grab one, that's your problem.

After couple of events, I moved to pole vaulting section and started warming up. The poles were made of bamboo and when I attempted my first jump, half way in the air, the pole cracked in the middle, but the momentum pushed me over the pole and I landed on the ground next to the edge of the padding. Besides being embarrassed and slightly shaken, I was OK. But the medics rushed to me and checked me all over. One of them noticed a lump on the right side of my belly, about the size of a walnut. I had it for some time. It did not hurt, so I left it alone.

So Monday, they took me to the surgical clinic for checkup and then they kept me in the hospital for surgery the next day. For my first time in a hospital, I was very apprehensive and a little bit scared. On the surgical bed, the doctor told me to count from one hundred and downwards, and started dripping some drops on me – ether – the most horrible smell, and I jumped and started fighting with the crew. And when they could not subdue me, they called for reinforcements, with about 5-6 people holding me, they put me to sleep. The next time I woke up, I was in the ward with some 12 other patients. The nurses kept coming and going changing bandages full with blood. When the doctor came to examine the wound, I was wrapped up with gauze all around my belly.

The doctor told me that they decided not to remove the tumor because it started profusely bleeding, but they took a biopsy which was sent to Krakow for analysis since they did not have a lab in Wroclaw to do it. "Meantime", I asked? Meantime, you will stay in the hospital until you heal and by then, we will have the results too. Now I know that ignorance is bliss, because at that time, I did not know any medical consequences, nor the dangers involved. The medical staff was very caring and the families of the other patients were amused at the foreigner being sick. They always used to bring me something to eat because they were subsidizing the nutritional needs of their loved ones. The result from Krakow came: "hemangioma simplex" or benign tumor.

In the meantime, I developed a tremendous tooth ache and some young lady dentist came to examine me. My two lower back teeth, were fully impacted with abscesses and Novocain would not work on abscesses. The doctor was concerned about infections, with a healing wound and an upcoming new surgery. So she said the teeth have to come out and warned me about the pain being involved. When my surgeon came to see me, I asked, "What pain doctor"? "There is nothing worse than ether being poured on you and I took it, did not I, doctor?"

He answered, "Yah, you took it all right, after 5 of us had to hold you down." So with those happy thoughts, the dentist took me to her office, and started chiseling the gums away to expose the teeth. Every second apologizing, "sorry it hurts". And I responded, "Doctor, don't talk, keep cutting, the faster the better." So the first tooth, she grabbed with the instrument, I heard cracking and felt pulling all the way to my legs. "How long those roots are, like it's giving me sort of electric shock all over."

So the first tooth is out, now we are working on the second. And again some chiseling, blood all over my face, the young dentist is scared and keep apologizing and grabs the tooth and pulls and I don't feel any roots cracking but she has part of the tooth in her instrument. And she starts crying because the stupid tooth broke in half and she panicked, confused with the outcome. So I grab her hands and with my mouth full of blood, calmed her down and told her not to worry, start working, chiseling, cutting, and pulling, because it has to be done, and don't stop until the tooth is out. I won't be hurting any more than it is now. How old was I – sixteen? Boy, I could be a good psychiatrist. So finally, about 2 hours of excruciating pain, the event was over.

Then I was in my bed, my body shaking, but gradually feeling better and better. The dentist stayed with me until the evening, making me comfortable, changing the cotton in my mouth and cleansing the face and continually apologizing.

A bunch of friends and the coach came to see me, and the coach, upon talking with the doctor, was happy and optimistic with the whole situation. And they brought me couple of oranges. Oranges in Poland, where the hell they stole them from!

Not far from the hospital was a performance arena. Saturday was approaching when the famous dance and song ensemble, Mazowsze were to perform. I asked the doctors if he can give me a pass to go and see Mazowsze because in a few days I will have the second surgery to remove the tumor. "Do you have a ticket?" the doctor asks. My reply was "No, but I will find some way to get inside." We had done this sort of thing hundreds of times and I was sure I would manage it somehow. So Saturday afternoon, the doctor sent a nurse to buy a ticket for me and instructed her how to prepare me, stuck a few zloty in my hand, and told me to be back by 12 midnight! I could kick myself, that I don't remember his name, I remember a few doctors names but who that was – nothing.

Before you enter our hospital room, you go through a hallway and of that hallway was a big door with partial glass and lead you to another room, where they treated more critical patients and among them 2 young, in their mid-twenties, fellows which were suffering from some cardiac ailments. I struck friendship with them and their families, which were coming to see them every day.

On the way to the concert, I stopped to say hello and being dressed in civilian clothes, they joked that they didn't recognize me. It was almost 3 weeks since I entered the hospital and it was so refreshing to get out of the hospital and breathe a fresh air. The concert was obviously fabulous and I enjoyed myself tremendously. By eleven o'clock, I was back in the hospital and passing through the hallway, opened the door to see my friends and some orderly stopped me. I could not go inside. I could see a very serious situation, bunch of doctors and nurses running around, oxygen tanks and other equipment and I thought that some of the older patient was in distress. However, the next morning, I learned one of my friends, the skinnier one with darker complexion, had died. That put me in an uncomfortable mood for days, and his parents and sister came to see me when they came to take his possessions.

My mouth healed after the dental adventure and this time they scheduled the second surgery. But this time the staff was prepared and tricked me to avoid another physical confrontation. All week ahead, I was uncomfortable and basically sick when I thought about the ether to put you to sleep. This time they put me on a normal bed, outside the surgery room, and said "here George, lie down and relax for a couple of hours" which postponed the agony that much. As soon I laid down, two husky guys jumped me, strapped me in the bed with leather straps, so I could not fight them. They put me to sleep first, then took me to the operating room.

The doctors cut the skin in shape of the letter L, pulled that skin up and cut the tumor from the inside of the skin and sewed me up. But the wound caught an infection and left such an ugly mark that I felt scarred and disfigured for all my life. It is not fair to do such damage to a beautiful body and I am telling you it was conspiracy all over. The incision was large and I was tightly wrapped. The doctors said not to walk for a few days. That put me somehow in an awkward situation, because lying down I could not urinate. I was too embarrassed to tell that to the staff and I also could not eat. The neighbor next to me, Mr. Kwiatkowski, noticed I am not eating and told the doctor. The doctor in turn started questioning me. And when I told him about urination difficulties, he immediately ordered catheterization and all kinds of vitamins. Upon installing the catheter, the nurse put a bottle on the floor so the tube will drain. Then the dam broke loose and the bottle filled up in a few seconds. I had to twist the tube to stop the flow and I had to call the nurse.

And she brought a new bottle and the second one filled in a few seconds and again I stopped the flow and again called the nurse. She brought the third bottle and again the situation repeated itself one more time. Three bottles were lined up on the floor, full of whatever came out of me and I felt deflated, like a balloon springing a leak and losing its air.

And I got scolded for keeping it quiet. The next day, totally unexpectedly, a visitor came in to see me. "Yes, it was my mother". How she managed to take the train and 3 hours drive in huge, strange city, and find the hospital is totally besides me, but nevertheless, here she is. The nurse brought her in and brought a comfortable chair for her. I explained in detail everything that had happened and that it was not dangerous and she calmed down. We spent all day together and one of the nurses was kind enough to take her to the train station and help her board the right train to Zgorzelec.

And about a week later I was discharged from the hospital, heavily bandaged and told to come back in 10 days for a checkup. Back in school, I was way behind in class and had to make up plenty of missed material with extra hours of studying and some tutorial help.

Then the second year was over, and I was home. I could not engage in any physical activities like sports or labor but managed to keep busy. My sister-in-law asked me to take her to Czechoslovakia, where her mother and sister lived, to see them. Her paperwork to go to Canada was still in progress and God knows when they would be able to see each other again. They lived in Sumperk close to my old stomping grounds, Sobotin. And we went to Sumperk, met with the family and few other relatives and friends. I took the train to Sobotin for a nostalgic visit and paid a visit to Mrs. Hajkova. Boy she was excited to see me, very happy that I made the effort to locate her. We spent a few hours together and she was up to date with my life. "I miss you terribly, you wild kids", she says, "now it's so quiet without you".

We stayed 10 days in Sumperk and then went back to Zgorzelec. In the meantime, the emigration situation was becoming frenzied. Greece started accepting some people back. Some started applying for visas to go to Yugoslavia, Macedonia, who had the same language, neighboring state to Greece; it is better having half loaf bread than nothing. But Yugoslavia would not issue any visas and the Bulgarian sharks, smelling blood in the waters, openly started issuing visas for all who wanted to go there. So many families rushed with their decision and moved to Bulgaria. Then Yugoslavia, somehow seeing the light and under Macedonian pressure, changed their policy and opened its borders and the flow toward Bulgaria stopped and everybody started going to Macedonia. The people who went to Bulgaria jumped from the frying pan into the oven, because letters started coming back to Poland and they were all negative and complaining about the shortages, economic and social conditions in Bulgaria. And since our family situation was different, we stood still.

My younger sister, Todora got married in Tashkent to a fellow also named George, and he had a sister in Macedonia. So in 1957, they moved from the god-forsaken Tashkent to the city of Prilep, Macedonia. Then mother, through the help of the local authority, applied for my sister, Vasilka to come to Poland and, lo and behold, my sister arrived in Zgorzelec in August 1957.

In 1958 I graduated from the technical school and any hopes of further education were sternly cut by mother. "Come home, she said, I need you here." My first cousin, also George, was living in the city of Legnica between Zgorzelec and Wroclaw, and he was applying to go to Greece to his wife and children. So while he was waiting for the documentation, mother took him home with us. Meantime, the papers came from Brother for his family to go to Canada. The logistics were staggering because all travel was conducted by train. My nieces, Terry and Mary were in school in the north of Poland.

To complete the process of leaving Poland, I made several trips to Wroclaw to submit applications and pick up the travel documents. We also went to Warsaw for physical exams, visas and tickets. So I had to arrange the trip for Pana to Warsaw one day later, so I can go to Szrecin to pick up my nieces and go to Warsaw, and meet Pana at the railroad station at a certain time, all along hoping that she did not miss any train. And all day going for interview in the Canadian embassy and the doctor's visit. Then putting back Pana on the train to Zgorzelec with a change in Wroclaw and me taking the nieces back, and then back home. And after a few more of those trips in December of 1958, my brother's family finally was delivered to the boat "Batory" in Gdansk, and took off for Halifax, Canada; one down, many to go.

After a few trips, Cousin George was dispatched in 1958 to Greece; two down. The immigration office for the region was in Wroclaw. This was where you would file your documents. There was a six-page questionnaire with 86 questions, where you had to answer every question. When you went to the window, a woman sat there and used a red pen to fill in what you missed. She told me the process the first time. You have to bring every document, you have to answer every question, and you cannot wait here and block the window. And if you are not prepared, you go home to get the correct documents. A reasonable demand from uncooperative bureaucrats, but then again that's how the bureaucracy sustains itself all over the world. Those documents they wanted were; a statement from your work place, that you really work there and notification to them that you would be leaving. A statement from the police department that they are aware of you leaving, a statement from the housing authority that you will leave the apartment and cannot give it to somebody else, but to the authorities only and as I said before, 86 questions have to be answered, from the most banal to the most important.

So having dispatched my brother's family to Canada, and cousin George to Greece, I was very familiar with the system and I had few packets of application papers with me so I could use them without going to Wroclaw to get them. In 1958, we brought to Zgorzelec, my sister's son Mial, from Czechoslovakia. She had not seen him for ten years, since he was three years old and left during the Civil War of 1948. I cannot describe this reunion in details because I will start crying, but picture yourself in the situation where you are forced to give up your 3 year old child and not seeing him for the next ten years, due to some mental deficiency of a few people addicted to the utopia, which in reality contradicts every thought and feeling, and then deprived of any humanity.

After couple of insignificant jobs for a short time, I started working for a huge construction company in charge of tracking and preparing their payroll. On the Polish side, in the triangle between Poland, Czechoslovakia and East Germany, a huge deposit of coal was discovered. All three countries were building a factory as a combined effort; a huge electricity producing plant. The word was that the East German designed the object; the Czechs were providing the machinery and the Polish, the labor force. The plant was located in the township of Thuroshow, not far from Zgorzelec, and our company was building housing and schools for many anticipating families who were coming to the region to fill the job openings. The Polish government issued a decree that any worker who had a perfect attendance record of work for the month would be paid an additional 25% to their regular salary because the production had to be on schedule, It is known fact that the alcoholism was rampant, hence the enhanced benefit of extra pay.

The payday was once a month (in cash) and the last week before the pay day was hectic for me, meetings with the technicians and foremen to get accurate days and hours, and deciding who got the bonus and who did not. I was getting many complaints about the accuracy of the work days, but I was directing all of them toward their foremen, since they were giving me the numbers. So every month, I would call a police escort to meet me at the post office (don't ask me why at the post office instead of the bank because I never figured it myself), pick up a huge canvas bag full of money, lock it to my wrist, give the key to the policeman, who took the manual calculator from the post office (bribery was involved) and go to my office, get the list from Mr. Makowski (I could not stand him as he was an arrogant and selfish person) put the table at the entrance door, butted to the wall, lock the window in the room, and as soon the siren sounded the end of the work day the cattle run started. People poured in to get paid.

Every last Friday of the month was the pay day and since we worked those days 6 hours on Saturdays, my boss Mr. Tabish, recognizing the efforts I put in and the abuse I took, let me take Saturday off. I had 14 guys – Macedonians including my friend Leon, working on the crew but sometimes they were heavier drinkers and missed more days than Polish workers. So the bonuses were cut. But during the deliberations of who gets cut on bonus, there were always some exceptions for some people having connections with the bosses. And the final list was signed by Mr. Tabish and that was the law. I requested from Mr. Tabish to give me two exceptions per month. He gave it to me, but asked me not to advertise it at the meetings because some foremen had personal grudges with my men. Just add the names last before I signed it, he said. So Leon was the beneficiary of my "generosity" and another fellow, who was drinking like a fish, but had 7 children to feed, and I did not have the heart to punish the kids. But on occasion when he had full month, I would "reward" some other compatriot.

Chapter IV   Reuniting the Family

Backtracking slightly, before my brother's family
left for Canada, my sister Todora, now living in
Macedonia, came to see us for a few weeks with her
son, Pascal, who was a toddler. So another short
period where we are still separated, but much closer
and the communication is flowing. Meantime, I was
very happy having a secure and well-paying job, and I
started doing the paperwork for my Aunt Ristana (my
Father's sister) whose husband and son were in
Youngstown, Ohio. And also the paperwork for my
sister Vasilka and Mial, going to Lorain to her
husband. So the fall of 1958 was full of travel and
many, many times, the overnight train to Warsaw was
so full, that I had to stand in the bathroom with other
people. If somebody had to use the bathroom, tough
luck.

Now, many years later, I get tired just thinking
about those times, but then it never bothered me.
Patience my man, patience. In July of 1959, I
dispatched my aunt and in August of 1959, my sister
Vasilka and Michael left for Lorain, Ohio. Suddenly,
only grandmother, mother and I were left and for the
first time I had my own room. On the political side, the
atmosphere was somehow looser, it was after the
Hungarian Revolution and an unpublicized incident in

Poznan. Where a group of factory workers revolted and seized a train full of ham and other meat products, which were going to exported while the Polish population was coping with empty shelves in the stores. The powers-that-be promised a few things, released Mr. Gormulka from jail, made him the head of government, and the more things changed, the more they stayed the same.

Before my sister left, she started calling me the "Secretary of State" with all the work I was doing for the family. But now, every day the biggest news in town was who got visas and to where. And my international services started growing, since many distant relatives of mother or friends started asking mother if I can help them with the paperwork. And mother never refused, many times I would come home from work and people would be at the apartment, waiting for me to come home. And I would always oblige them, and many, if not all, would pull money out to pay me, but I would never, never, accept any penny. Well, once I took compensation. The guy with 7 children, I was instrumental so he gets the bonus. He was a distant relative of my sister-in-law and since they could not go any place, so they decided to go to Bulgaria. There was no need for me to do any paperwork for Bulgaria, but upon coming home, there she was, his wife, waiting for me.

There was international radio transmission from Macedonia and they would play Macedonian songs. You could write in and ask them to play any song and dedicate it to whomever you wanted. So the Macedonian records were in huge demand and this lady had the best collection. So when I came home, she was in and very comfortable with my mother. "You need some help, I asked"? "No", she said, "you helped me many times to feed my children, with the bonus you were giving to my husband, although he did not deserve it". (I had told him, if ever the word leaks out, I'll stop the bonus, because everybody will demand it) and she proceeded, so-and-so want to buy my records, and I don't like them, and I thought about you, how much you did for us and I want you to have the records as an appreciation and I will never forget your help. So how can I argue with such reasoning; I accepted the full case of records, all 18 of them.

There was one lady, frail, and very timid. Her husband was serving in the army with my brother so she was well acquainted with my sister-in-law and mother. One morning in the market, she started conversation with my mother and they discussed the news that yesterday 18 notifications had arrived from the Greek embassy in Warsaw. So most of them sort of celebrated and bragged about the news, but this scared lady tells mother that not 18 people, but 19 people, got the papers. "Who is the 19th?", mother asked. And she confirmed that she was the 19th person, but kept that confirmation quiet until she talked with mother. Obviously mother is very happy and invites her home, so she can talk with the "Secretary of State". When I came home, the woman was very shy and apologetic. She showed me the papers that stated she has to respond within 6 months to Greek embassy with her intentions.

All the paper applications were in Greek and you had to go in-person to the Greek embassy, but first you had to go to Wroclaw to get the Polish approval. So after making her comfortable, I explained the whole procedure. "Oh no", she says, "the whole group wants to go". "They want to go to Wroclaw within a week and I want to go with them. I am not capable to go alone." "Listen", I said, "you go to all of these offices, get all the statements and bring them to me, then I will fill out the 86 questions", (which I could do while sleeping, as they were the same questions for everybody). People are going every day in Wroclaw so I will connect you with somebody. A few days later, she meets mother on the street and expresses concern, as nobody else from the group knows about having these documents. Besides who is doing your paperwork coming with this silly requirements and mother, being a very sure motivator, reassured her to do what I told her. So two weeks later, all 19 go to Wroclaw and all 18 come back with the rejected applications, except my "client." I was so happy and proud that I listened to you, she tells me when the rest were stunned and commiserating that nobody succeeded, especially the loud braggers. After she left for Greece, her husband sent me a beautiful letter with thanks and compliments that I am like my brother.

And in the meantime, what happened to the 18 rejects? Why we have a "Secretary of State" in the town. All of them, in groups as relatives, or individually, came to me and I was glad to oblige them. A few of the more obnoxious ones insisted on paying me and stuffed the money in my hand or pocket, but I am sure that they did it to satisfy their egos, rather than for my work. I was living on the 4th floor and my friend, Leon was on the 1st floor. One day upon coming home from work, I found Leon's grandmother waiting for me, and she showed me piece of paper from the post office notifying her that a packet was waiting for her at the post office. She had a daughter in Tashkent (so it was from her), and since Leon was working late, she asked me to go with her to get the packet.

"Let's go", I said, and we went to the post office. Everybody knew me there through work or personal business. The postal workers had a few questions to fill out on the paperwork. Name, no problem?, Address, no problem? Date of birth - big problem. She was in her late seventies and totally illiterate. "Grandma, do you know when you were born?", I asked. "Yes", she replied as I stood ready to translate the date to the postal girl. "I was born the year when the huge lightning struck the big poplar tree and uprooted it." And I burst out laughing and asked her if she was sure it was uprooted, and how she remembered it, since she was so small when she was born. "Come on George, what is the joke", Elizbieta says, and laughs because I am laughing. Hold it a second, instead of in number, I will tell you in words, and my laugh is accelerating, as a couple of other clerks joined in. Ready for DOB? And I tell them the time she was born but nobody is old enough to verify that fact. And still laughing made her put an X on the signature line and the girls getting the joke, started laughing and I had to leave before she pops some other gem. And afterwards, for weeks, the girls carried on every time I borrowed their calculator. And the day was coming when Leon, his mother, grandmother and two younger brothers were going to leave and go to Greece, where his father was.

A few other friends had already left for various countries and although we were writing to each other, I missed them terribly. Vangel had gone to Macedonia,

Lazo, upon graduation got a job in Wroclaw, (his father was killed in the Civil War of 1949), and his mother got remarried to some Greek fellow, but Lazo could not stomach it and kept his distance. Vasil was there and both of us started packing up Leon for Greece. At that time, you would lease a railroad car. They would put it on the side and you could pack all your furniture, bicycles, motorcycles, etc. and when you were ready, the rail people would come, seal the car and ship it to any city in the country you were going to.

So the day came to part with Leon and Vasil and I went with him and his family up to Gliwice, the last stop before the train enters Czechoslovakia. And yes, it was a very sad situation parting with the best friends but, at least it was the reverse of splitting from families. This time, the families were re-uniting. Leon promised to write me right away, but two months went by until I heard from him. And then I got a packet from Leon and he sent me a Greek wine, olives, (which in Poland they did not know what it is), some dry garbanzo beans and boxes of raisins. Typical native stuff, which we did not have since we left. Then he was drafted into the army, kept sending me letters and pictures, but the family situation with the father did not pan out. However, all three brothers stuck it out with their mother and grandmother. After the stint in the army, he started work in construction and was running a big crew, building roads. Then I got pictures from his wedding. He had married a beautiful local teacher in the city of Kostur.

So from the old band of musketeers from Czechoslovakia, Vasil and I were in Zgorzelec and Vasil with his father, sister and three other brothers, decided to go to Macedonia. Our status was that as long as grandmother is alive, we will suffer, and never abandon grandmother. And Vasil's family were not in a hurry to go, some had time to finish their jobs, buy some items (motorcycles, etc.)

In the fall of 1960, grandmother did not feel herself. Something was bothering her and she called me; "tell your mother when she comes home to see me". She was staying in the back of the apartment in her own room. But you have to go through the kitchen to her room. Mother or I were delivering the meals on the table in her room and she had developed a sixth sense to navigate with the utensils, cups and dishes. Many times during the dinner, she would ask for a glass of water. I would put it next to a smaller glass with alcohol. She very much enjoyed an occasional drink and I made sure that she got it more often than not. Upon drinking the alcohol, she always commented with the same statement: "Ack – grandma's golden boy, now you make my meal perfect."

So as soon as mother came home, I told her to go and see her. After a few minutes with grandmother, she called me, that we have to move her in the living room, on front of the apartment where there was much more daylight. And then mother sent me to bring 3 older ladies to our place, which I knew them well, and to the certain degree were related to our family. When they came, mother sent me to go my friend's house to stay there overnight, because I don't belong there. And then some more women came and stayed overnight and by next day before noon, my grandmother died. Even mother did not know exactly how old she was but by reckoning and comparing different events in the past, the consensus was that she was well over 80 years old.

While mother and other ladies were changing grandmother, I went to the, the, I don't know where, this was new territory for me. And notified the department of "the dead people"? That afternoon, the funeral carriage came with a casket, put grandmother on the carriage and the procession started toward the cemetery. And the word spread fast. And the people started lining behind the carriage and the ordinary citizens stopping on the streets, praying and the men removing their hats and all of this sounded so surrealistic, so many strange people, not knowing grandmother at all, paying her such respect. For a couple of weeks, I was real down, it was difficult to get used to an empty house.

Every time, when coming home, I would open the kitchen door and holler: "are you OK grandma?" And she, like waiting for me with a happy voice, would respond: "The devil can take me as long you are OK." So another chapter in the family life was closed. The matriarch of the family is gone. However, the forces which run this planet never stop. They are on their job constantly and that is why we have sunny days and rainy days, for every tear dropping from somebody's eyes, is compensated ten-fold with somebody's beautiful smiles. And the clock of life keeps ticking and we are adjusting to whatever is coming.

By mid-December, I started experiencing some pain in my right leg, starting from the pelvic area and shooting down through my thigh. Comes and goes but one day it was so intense that my boss ordered me to go to the hospital for checkup. I walked to the hospital (my limo was at the shop) and upon taking some blood samples and other tests, they determined that it is appendicitis. They kept me overnight, and the next morning prepped me for surgery. Vividly remembering the my previous fiasco with ether, I ask the doctor if he can do it with local anesthetic. He agreed. They numbed the area, started working on me and carrying their conversations like they are at the market. "O.K.

Where it is?" the doctor says, and started twisting my insides. I was thinking he will pull my lungs out, it was so painful. "Ah, there it is", and snips and shows me some ugly thing. "You are lucky", he says, "it was almost ready to rupture on you." I said, "Thank you very much." The nurse helped me get up from the table saying, "Sorry we don't have a wheelchair". She held onto me by my left arm, and I held the wound with my right hand. And we walked from the operating table to the end of the hallway, where my bed was, a distance of about 50 yards. So far so good, I said to myself, the stitches still hold, what else do you want.

After the initial expected pain, the thing started healing but they kept me two weeks there, thanks to the social medical system. However the next morning after surgery, the nurse pops in, cheerfully open the curtains, and says "Can you help me honey in the next room?" "Sure, why not?" I answer. We go to the next room, where a gurney is waiting next to the bed and we grab the body of a dead patient and flip him on the gurney. "Thank you sweetie", she says and goes with the dead person. By the time I realized what had transpired, everything was finished, the nurse gone, and the dead person was gone. I went to my room and washing my hands, thinking, did that really just happen? Yes, it happened. But in those days that's how things were run.

Our street was saturated with stoic tall buildings, 5-7 stories each connected to the other and since people started moving to different countries, new people were settling in, which made the character of the neighborhood start changing. Most of us immigrants were concentrated in several blocks, close to each other, therefore everybody knew each other – the older men were socializing together on the outside benches, around the fountain on the side of the main road "Ulica Dzierszynskieg" which spanned the city from one end to the other. The women communicated by opening the windows and hollering to each other or meeting on the street, and/or going to the markets together and the whole neighborhood had sort of free, ethnic atmosphere.

The new people from Polish agricultural areas, Bytom-Kielece or Krakow, were coming to get new jobs at the new electric plan in Turoshow, and were assigned the apartments that our people were leaving. There was very strict inventory of the apartments causing the two cultures to mix together. And somehow a sort of resentment developed in the minds of the elderly Macedonians. However, it was the new Polish arrivals, who were affected much more negatively! Leaving their places, where they grew up, coming to a new, much bigger city, starting new jobs in the industrial sector and abandoning farming. On top of that, they were being settled among populations foreign to them, and being looked upon like they are the "foreigners" was not easy. And my generation was maturing, and getting the benefits of the system, yet we had not been drafted for the military and that created resentment on the part of the population.

List of Pictures (by page)

Збогум, родна земјо: евакуацијата на Македончињата од Егејска Македонија

93

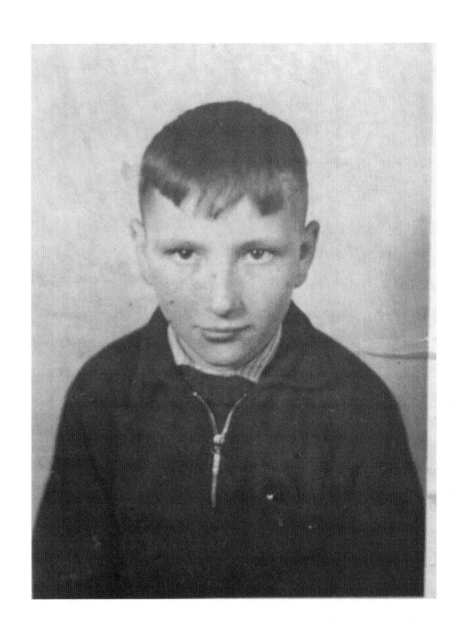

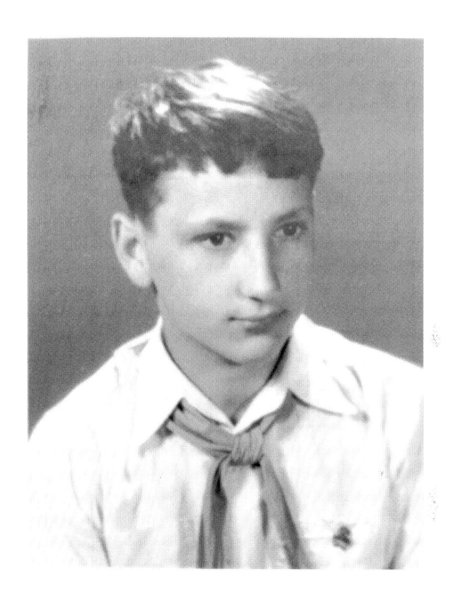

98

106

111

128

Chapter V   Being Macedonian

In the spring of 1961, my father had sent papers to the American embassy in Warsaw and we were waiting to hear from them. And the call came, so now mother was part of the "State Department Operations." The novelty of being a political refugee after a few years wore off on the tired Polish people since they were the first receivers of the German brutality and were now being controlled by the Russian colossus. So the tempers ran short sometimes. When you have to compete for jobs or apartments with some strange foreign people, the situation gets tense.

So the timing was perfect for us to proceed in different direction in our lives. For me, being in Zgorzelec was a necessary move, due to the family circumstances and I sacrificed too much for that reason, interrupting my higher education. My aspiration was to emigrate to the United States. Some of my friends achieved their dreams to be engineers, doctors, artists, etc. and they were content to stay there. America then and now is the biggest magnet, which draws people from all over the world, and me being young, father has been here since 1938 and working in Bethlehem Steel and then opening a business, I was not worried at all, I can still achieve my dreams in America. Although there were several "emissaries" coming to talk to mother from good families, about those prearranged marriages, that was the furthest thing from my mind. First, I was too young for marriage, and secondly – brother and father were warning me not to marry, because it will change the status of qualifying for a visa to U.S.A. And although father and brother worried, they did not know that sister had bestowed on me, the title of "Secretary of State" and I was fully aware of all rules and regulations when it came to emigration.

What I was not aware of, though, was the perfidy the Greek government snuck on us from far away. In late fifties, Poland and Greece singed agreement for trade, cultural exchange, tourism, etc. Soon after, Greek goods started appearing in the stores, figs, wine, olives, peppers, etc. They also agreed, unknown to us Macedonians and Poland, I think, not knowing the nuances of the Greek politics and attitudes toward Macedonian minority, that any Macedonian living Poland and going to America, Canada, Australia, cannot get Polish exit visas until they go through the Greek embassy in Warsaw and get a special permit to show the Polish, in order to get the exit visas. Certainly you have heard about the adage "Beware of Greeks bearing gifts." Well that comes from the glory years before B.C. era, where Greece dominated the Earth in everything scientific, military, building and tricked the enemy in Troy with the wooden horse. The dominance of the Greek hegemony in those above years is indisputable and forms the basis for the modern medicine, architecture and other scientific subjects. And as the world evolves, other dynasties came along and dominated the scene and disappeared.

Greece was under Ottoman Empire for over 500 years and lost huge amount of territory to the Turks. Being under someone's domination for so many years, obviously going to lose not only territory, but also influence in the region. Once you inspired it, controlled it and dominated it. In Europe, there is no country that can say that "we are one people, one nation, one blood brothers, expect maybe in the Scandinavian nations. The populace kept moving, the stronger could conquer the weaker nations, and if you could put a marker on the spot and declare this is our nation, this is going to be only geographical divide, the population is divided on both sides of the maker so the Slavs came in the Balkans at various times; through history and settled in the empty spaces in Macedonia, Bulgaria, Serbia and so forth. They did not displace any other races.

Let's get to the modern times: Greece is a small country (territory-wise and has about 10 million people at present. Turkey is about 80 million people and much bigger in size. However, the ego of the Greek ruling class never adjusted to the present reality. They associate with the big boys, England and France, Germany, with huge royal weddings and parties, all over the credit of the past brilliance! The workers, the peasants were left on their own, as long as the rich played the Royalty card. At periods of time, they were ruled by kings and some periods of times by the military rulers. When Macedonians, who were totally neglected (about 1 million of them) and abandoned by the Greek governments, rebelled in the 1900s to get rid of the Turks and create an independent Macedonian state, the Greeks awakened and used their influence with England, to divide Macedonia into 3 sections. The biggest part took Greece, then Serbia and smallest, Bulgaria. So Macedonia went from small to smaller. And then the terrorizing of the people started. Greeks sent teachers to teach the Greek language to the populace, started enforcing laws to curtail the freedom, put an embargo on not speaking the Macedonian language and not to be able to sing any Macedonian songs. They started bringing people from Asia Minor to dilute the ethnicity of the Macedonians and pretending and lying to the different humanitarian organizations that there are not minorities in Greece. The Greeks are astute businessmen and hard-working entrepreneurs and have been manipulated and lied to by mostly western educated politicians playing on the psyche about the past history. That was the reason Greece inserted the demand for all Macedonians to pass through the Greek embassy.

Greece with its unjustified insistence about non-existing minorities and blocking the newly world-wide recognized state of Macedonia, which was part of former Yugoslavia, to enter the international organizations is reinforcing the absolute truth that there is really a Macedonian minority in Greece. Nowadays, you cannot put a Trojan horse through and fool the world. With the Greek know-how, business acumen, and smartness – yes - still left from the glory years, Greece can become regional powerhouse economically among their neighbors, forget the past atrocities, with Bulgarian and Turks, open the borders so your neighbors can see the beautiful islands and the past historical places, give full freedom to speak and write their languages to the Macedonians of northern Greece.

Thessaloniki used to be Solun, Florina used to be Lerin, Kastoria used to be Kostur and Michaelidis used to be Miovski. And you don't have to kiss the German ass to back you out of misery which you created on your own by playing politics with the big boys. Greece could become the Switzerland of the

Balkans if it adopts some strong working ethical behavior and fiscal discipline and started implementing the existing laws and strengthening where is need to collect all the taxes due from everybody, especially from the rich, and educated elite, instead of depending mostly on the workers. At least try to curtail the corruption by putting few tax evaders and politicians to jail and apply the law uniformly to all, so the masses can wake up and start believing in the government.

Above all stop abusing the minorities, reconstitute the word "democracy" remember? You invented it in the glory past. And make every step transparent so people can be free and accountable for their deeds. Right now, Greece is in existence as a third world country despite billions of dollars in foreign aid from America and the West. And who am I that is preaching these theories? I am a lifelong Greek citizen who happened to be a member of the minority Slavic Macedonians. And for that reason, I am being persecuted, changed my name to an unknown Greek name, ejected from Greece, property confiscated, regardless that my family lived there for centuries and my brother Spiro served the Greek army.

So what are you afraid of, Greece? The Macedonians should be put on the pedestal because most of the food you have is grown in Macedonian fields. And yet, you, the so-called powerful country, are afraid of your shadow. I wonder what the glorious predecessors will think about you if they see you somehow, that you – Greece – inheriting so much from them and let it slip through your sticky fingers. Shame on you.

So mother and I go to Warsaw. To ease the overnight trip for her I bought a first class ticket to avoid the possibility of standing all night in the hallways. First thing in the morning we go to the doctor's office for checkup. Then we go to Sabena Airlines to pick the tickets and finally we go to Greek embassy for the papers to get the exit visa. It was March 25th, a Greek national holiday, the liberation from Turkish dominance. After a few polite words, they showed us a table with olives, feta cheese, coffee, some crackers. Please help yourself, it is our holiday they said, implying that we are part of celebration. Thirteen years passed since I left Greece and there is not one iota of interest on the government part, are we OK, alive, dead? After all, we are supposed to be Greek children, according to them. Don't you care about thirty-thousand children? No, all they care is to neutralize the Macedonian identity, so if you go to the western countries, America, Canada, Australia, you are not carrying the Macedonian mark or any indication of your true heritage.

I am called into the office of a Greek officer and asked the following questions. Your name? George Miovski. Date of birth and place of birth? April 28, 1939, village Orovo, Prespa. Ahem, let me check up and pulls out a book with handwritten content. "Why don't you want to go back to Greece instead of to America?", he arrogantly asks. "Why would I go to Greece? Since I have nobody there, where would I stay when my father is in America?" "Well you have a point, but here I have all records of your village, and I don't see any last name like you are telling me who you are. I have a person by first name of George born the same day you are but, the family name is not what you are telling me. The name is Michaelidis and you have older brother in Canada, also Michaelidis.

I am sitting there feeling like a trapped animal, trying not to blow it and, yet, I am boiling with anger, but I have to respond to him. Since I was born, and left Greece at age of 8 and up to now, going through Czechoslovakia and Poland and nobody, not my family at home and through schooling in both countries *ever* called me by that name. And all my documentation it is written "Miovski" and now you are telling me that this is the wrong name?

"Well, we don't have influence in other countries, but in Greece you are Michaelidis, and if you want to go to America, that is your correct name." So now what would you, dear reader, do in this situation? Would you play stubborn and throw away the chance to reunite with your father who you've never seen, or accept the other name, which was imposed on us in the 1930s before I even was born. I did not have anybody with me to consult, and I could not play a hero and ruin the chance of unifying with my father and, above all, messing up the chance to come to America. America was the Promised Land for millions of people from the beginning of the 20th century, but through the peak of the Cold War and living under the savagery of Russia, people in Eastern Europe had multiplied their affinity toward the Americans. So I accepted the fate thrown upon me by the snooty snobbish official, got the paperwork and grabbed a taxi to the bank so we could buy 5 American dollars each for the long and long-awaited journey to the one and only America. Why only 5 dollars? Because the government was hoarding the foreign currency, and had a huge apparatus of agents to support and terrorize the people.

After that we went to the train station for the all night ride to Wroclaw. We stopped in Wroclaw for a few hours to see a relative. In the meantime, I ran to the passport office and had the exit visas stamped on the traveling documents and America, here I come. We had a window of six months to leave Poland and that gave us a breathing room to prepare, dispose of various items and say goodbye to our friends. It is a custom that close friends and relatives drop by to say safe trip and goodbyes. But mostly, I received complaints about who would handle their immigration papers. The "Secretary of State" was closing the office. But a few elderly ladies I had in the pipeline were assured, because I had them connected with another fellow who was an electrician and commanded the Polish language quite well.

While I was preparing to leave, Vasil's family was almost ready and we set the date we are leaving, April 1, and Vasil, a week later because he insisted coming to Warsaw to send me off. I gave all my stuff and clothing to my friends. I had one suitcase with books and family pictures and was wearing a new blue shirt and pants. I had never flown on a plane, and I was very apprehensive and every time a plane was flying above, I would look at it thinking how the heck I would fly that high without filling my pants. And then a plane crashed, I think in France, and all passengers perished in the accident. And I had to keep it secret from my mother. And then one afternoon, on the last day of March, a huge group of friends, boys and girls, surrounded me and mother (behind us were her relatives) and we all started marching toward the train station.

A couple of teenage girls – I was good friends with their brothers, started crying, please take us to America! If it was that easy. To avoid any kind of sentimentality, I hopped on the train and Vasil escorted mother and few minutes later, the train took off. Eight years before the same train brought me to Zgorzelec, and now I am getting nostalgic, thinking back. Eight years ago, a boy comes to this country to start an interrupted life with his mother, and now, a 22 year old man goes again to a strange country to meet his father for the first time. However, the stakes now were much higher. For the last time, I am glancing around familiar terrain then slowly the train picked up full speed and Zgorzelec disappeared from my view. But not from my mind because it was there where I matured, built up my character, met and responded to the many challenges that made me who I am today.

In Wroclaw, we changed trains for the all night ride to Warsaw. Mother mostly tried to catch some sleep but I was all in knots, very nervous talking with Vasil about everything and thinking about one thing – how am I going to respond when I meet my father. Several times in Zgorzelec, when I was alone, going to work, I tried to pronounce loudly the word "father" with different strength and value, but I was not able to judge it on my own. We also discussed at length, Vasil's situation, as he was also starting new life in the different country – Macedonia, Yugoslavia · but at least he was going to a country where they speak the same language. The only word of English I knew and that from the movies, was "mister." So how can you get lost in a new country, when half of the population you can address by the title? Ya, it's funny now, but then, I was sweating bullets.

The next morning, the train arrives in Warsaw. For Vasil, it is his first time in Warsaw, but I know the city upside down. After refreshing myself in the beautifully kept public facilities, I took them (don't forget I have mother with me) to the "S" Class restaurant, right on the premises of the train station. It was greatly appointed and served excellent food, with the mind of serving foreign travelers. It was also expensive, but then I am already part American. I had plenty of zloty left, so after paying the bill, I bought the return ticket for Vasil and gave him the rest of the Polish money. We took a taxi to the airport, (it is 12 o'clock) and the plane is coming from Moscow to Brussels at about 1 o'clock. After a short time, the plane lands, and is rolling up on the runway with tremendous noise and, I again freeze upon seeing the mechanical monster, a French-made Caravelle jet. I touched my rear end and it was still dry, so we hugged and kissed, (both crying) and started boarding. After less than 2 hours of flying, still filled with anxiety, we land in Brussels. A lady agent from Sabena Airlines takes us to the boarding area for N.Y., seated us on the chairs, points to the clock to give us the time, and shows as the direction to board. Then goes to the lady behind the counter, points toward us and talks to her co-worker. The other lady looks at us, waves with a smile.

And I feel much better already that we are under someone's care, but I can't answer all questions asked by mother, such as where are we, why did they put us here to wait, what did lady say who was speaking to me, since she did not understand her language. It was all Greek to me as well! So the loudspeaker started announcing some things, people started getting up, the Sabena employee came to us, took the boarding passes to N.Y. and pointed to the gate with a smile. Within two hours in the airport we got more smiles than in Poland for a whole year. And in no time we are streaming toward N.Y. in an incredible huge jet, Boeing 707. The previous night going to Warsaw and all day going through the motions, I was exhausted and fall asleep for few hours, but the pilot started talking and woke me up. I looked through the window and I can see lights below which meant we had crossed the Atlantic, and are now over American soil.

I explained this to mother, but I am sure that she is going through some difficult emotions and feelings on her own. It has been 24 years since father departed and through all the terrible times; the second World War, the civil war, deportation to Poland, her separation from my sisters, brothers, and me, she endured more pressure and hard luck than the average person could handle. And she had to care for grandmother on top of that. She was not an ordinary

143

person. She was dedicated to the family to the utmost and worked long hours, taking care of the livestock, and planting the fields and, at harvest time, plowing. She organized the work and hired the people to harvest the crops, (since my brother was in the Army). Pana, my sister in law, was working next to her. The two women were dealing with the difficult circumstances much better than many families with men.

One summer, being home from school in Zgorzelec, mother and I were coming home from the store. At the meeting place on the street, (where the water fountain was), a person from our village saw us and crossed the street to talk to mother. He asks, "Hi George, home for the summer?" I answer, "Yes." And he asks mother if she can sell him few American dollars? The dollars were in huge demand and father or brother were sending her a few dollars on occasion, (which mother would always keep). And there were specialty stores where you can buy foreign goods, but only with hard currency. And mother answers him: "Yes, I have American and Canadian dollars but you would be the last person on earth that I would sell them to and even not then". What was that all about I ask my mother. "There were four men in the household, him, his two sons and his brother. They did not have their own land and during harvest time, we always hired him to help and were paying them well. The last harvest year, your brother and sisters were gone, only Pana and I were there and I approached him to come and help with his sons and he turns me down." He said "why your son is in the Army and husband in America. Let them come down and help you." She answered him, "but before they were gone also, but you came and we helped you making money". These were different times, he tells mother, now the Communism is coming. I was overwhelmed the by the way mother handled him and embarrassed when he left. So mother had paid her dues in sweat, in pain, in worrying, and now a new chapter is awaiting her, and hopefully will be much easier than up to now.

I looked through the window and I cannot believe what I am seeing. From far, I see millions of lights as we are approaching the landing. An unbelievable galaxy of lights, different colors, buildings, streets, advertising, and everything twinkles, blinks, jumps at you, in a tantalizing display of unimaginable fantasy and it strikes me somehow, that yes, Virginia, there is a city named New York. The city we hear of millions of times, we had seen the skyline of buildings, reaching the clouds, so many times in the American movies, documentaries, and the Empire State Building, yes I can see it, you can't miss it, the tallest!

I pointed to mother to look and see it, and she sort of panics and asks, "it is the abyss?" No mother, it is New York, the one and only. She questioned, "We are not going to live here are we?" I answered, "No mother, we are going to Buffalo." The plane landed and we went through Customs and who is going to bother a young fellow and an elderly lady looking like peasants and acting like ones, turning our heads left and right, and absorbing the energy generated by the pace of life. Everything was new, everything was exciting, so many people, everything was overwhelming. There were so many blacks, both men and women, working and helping. This was the first time I saw so many black people congregating in an enclosed area. As we were entering the general area, from Customs, a young black lady sees us and asks – "George?" She did not address me as "mister", and I did not know how to respond and just blurted Ahem! "Welcome to America", she says with a smile and extends her hand to shake our hands. I see the Sabena Airlines logo on her lapel, so she is with the airlines.

So I was happy knowing that we were under the full control of the airline agents. She seated us and emphasized with her hands that we were to stay seated and she left the area. In the meantime, I am seeing the airport employees, airline passengers, young people traveling, some hugging, separating, and

146

moving about. The automatic doors were constantly opening and closing and to me it was total chaos, how these people navigate? A stupid idea crosses my mind and I am going to give it a try. In Czechoslovakia they taught us that blacks are discriminated at public places and yet here are so many blacks working. Let me watch the automatic doors to see if they are going to open for the blacks. And sure enough, the doors open and again and again and I think, at least the doors are not discriminating. Meanwhile, the black lady helping us comes with a golf cart, puts us on and drives us to a far wing where we are going to board the plane to Buffalo. And I see the sign – Buffalo.

Well, we are not in Kansas anymore, I mean Zgorzelec. We boarded the American Airlines plane to Buffalo, but it was not a jet, just a propeller plane, and then we were in the air. Buffalo, here we come. Later, when we landed in Buffalo and were going toward the exit, my heart was pounding in my chest, wanting to go back. But, back where? There is no back anymore.

As we enter the public zone, I spotted my brother and recognized him right away and next to him, a shorter person in a dark suit and hat with a typical American belly, like we used to see in the American movies. And when I saw his face, sure enough, he is my Father. The resemblance to my brother was undeniable. My brother ran and hugged me. Mother

147

and Father met, but did they kiss? Father (as I learned later) is not the kissable type. Then father comes to me with one arm, hugs me and the other arm sort of hits me in the back. Some artificial tears dropped and he handed me a gift. A cigar lighter, one of those fancy Zippos. He said, "I did not know if you smoke, but here all the young men smoke and drink." Obviously, I was not a smoker or drinker but so far so good. I can do it if I want to.

We got into my brother's car, (a black Ford Fairlaine), and started driving. I did not know if my father had a house or what. My brother takes us in South Buffalo on Buffum Street where father had rented a second floor apartment, with big rooms plenty of space. I am totally exhausted after such a long trip; an all night train ride, then the flight to Brussels, then the long flight to New York City with the final stop – Buffalo. It is 11 o'clock evening and brother takes me to downtown, where he had reserved a room at Buffalo Hotel on Seneca Street. After the cordial questions and answers between both of us, about his family, his girls, about me, my sleep was gone and I was so happy to be with my brother, that we talked most of the night. The appearances are misleading brother tells me. "Father is not what mother is, and many years apart turned him to be on the cold side family-wise. I told him so many times to bring me to U.S.A – with anticipation

148

that you will come. We could go into business together, but he would not hear it, wanting to be alone. So you are going to have a rough time ahead, but learn English and, if you want to come to Toronto, I'll bring you. But I want to make it clear, I can't live with father in the same house. "So listening to this characterization of my father, my mirage of my future disappeared fast and sobered me faster. In the morning we went to the house on Buffum Street where mother makes breakfast overwhelmed with the new gadgetry in the kitchen. After that, my brother again takes me out, this time to Seneca Street. He bought me a new watch (a Bulova), some underwear, and a shirt. When I protested that I had bought a new shirt in Zgorzelec, he said, 'No, that is the kind of shirt the bus drivers wear here". O.K. new shirt it is. Then my brother left for Toronto.

Mother and father had plenty to talk about, the village, the property, what happened to this and that, but were not willing to touch the "second phase" of our lives, after we left Greece. Gradually I learned that father proscribed to the theory of Macedonia being Bulgaria. There was an organization, the Macedonian Patriotic Organization (MPO), which was heavily influenced by Bulgarian government since Macedonia was the dedicated Grand Prize for whoever succeeded to grab her in their influence; Bulgaria or Greece or

Serbia. The MPO leaders had their headquarters in Spain and with annual MPO conventions and a weekly newspaper, coming out of Indiana, somebody was making very cushy living out of those who were uneducated, naïve and starved for belonging to something close to the homeland. However, the whole generation of father's age were somehow suppressed, scared of the system, misinformed about the external situations. They were uneducated and restricted to communicating in the English language only partially and phonetically. As a result, they were missing many opportunities available to them and any news coming to their attention was incorrectly understood or twisted to their wishes. They could talk all day without solving or agreeing on anything. However, some of them had smarts and done well for themselves. In many instances by taking advantage of their countrymen.

In 1962, when we come to Buffalo, father was approaching 65 years old. He had a business, a bar and restaurant with a partner on Seneca Street named Seneca Grill. Prior to our arrival, he somehow got sick and sold his share for $14,000. I don't know how the business was run but meeting his partner only once, (when father took me there), I guarantee you that father was being taken advantage of. $14,000 at that time was a big sum of money, however that is all father had to his name. The weekly or monthly income was spent on his upkeep rent and annual visits to the MPO convention in various cities every year. In the meantime, not having a steady income coming in, I knew his nest egg would disappear in no time. Common sense tells me to find a job, but the practical situation presented itself in such a way that I could not figure out how to solve it. I know absolutely nobody, I do not have transportation, I do not know the language, but I desperately need job. I sat down with father and express my concerns. He started crying about the turns of events and explained to me that he put in a bid for another bar and grill and was waiting for an answer. When I heard that I started crying, but out of desperation. I had seen some of his bar customers drinking and smoking, and I did not want to fall in that kind of lifestyle.

I left the house and walked to Seneca Street where on the left, a few yards down, I see a park – Cazenovia Park. I turned toward the park and heard big noises and cheering. I followed the sounds and on that beautiful April day, found a field with a huge group of adults who were cheering, small kids playing some stupid game, dressed in some funny uniforms and hats, holding some huge gloves, and bats, running around. I sit on an empty bench and try to make some sense of the game, but I don't get it. My thoughts went

151

to the past, playing soccer, participating in track meets, when Leon, Vasil and Lazo, and other friends we got together. I wondered how they are coping with their situations. They landed in much worse countries than I. So I went back home and asked father how much time it would take to buy the bar and grill. Six to seven months he says, as it takes time to get a liquor license.

The next day, father takes me to downtown on the bus, and on Main Street, he introduces me to the owner of Andreff's Restaurant, Tome. Tome was a big husky guy, bald, but very friendly. We talk, and he gave me a milk shake and tells father, "Alex, I did not know you have such a handsome son." "Neither did I", responded father.

When we left the restaurant, father tells me "why don't you stay here longer, scan the city and when you want to come home, walk to Seneca Street and take the bus # (whatever it was), and depart at Buffum, you know the neighborhood. Yes, I surely know it, being here less than a week. He gave me a $10 bill, and said, "if you are hungry, go to Tome's and eat. So I am sort of window shopping, gaping at every window to kill some time. At one window, I hear two guys talking some Slavic language, but it is not Macedonian or Serbian; a dialect I had not heard. I followed them some distance but still couldn't recognize the language.

What the heck do I have to lose, I thought, and approached them directly asking, "Where are from, guys?" Macedonia was the reply. I said but you speak with a different accent. We are from Strumica and have very distinctive accent, but also speak Macedonian. "I am George", I said, and I came here from Poland a week ago". We all went back to Andreef's Restaurant, where they practically controlled the traffic, since they are close with the owner. Then they explained me that there is a large immigration pool of Macedonians, Greeks, Polish, Italians here in Buffalo and that the restaurant is practically their headquarters of a sort. One guy's name was Stojan and the other's Blagoja. And then came many others: Mitko, Radko, and George (all from Strumica, a city in Macedonia). I got lots of news about the city of Buffalo and places to work, and they walked me to the bus saying, "come back tomorrow, somebody is always here".

Going home, I was taken aback with all the advertising on the bus and started trying to make any sense of it. The words were difficult and I could not pronounce them. But my mood changed when I realized that I am not alone. All kinds of people had recently arrived in the United States. When I reached home, I told father about being unable to pronounce one word of the bus advertising. I asked him if there is a sort of schooling in the English language since we would have a few months before acquiring the bar. And father said, "Sure, there is the International Institute on Delaware Avenue. Those are the people who made the papers for you and mother to emigrate here".

The next day, we took the Seneca Street bus to Main Street, then walked a short distance and took the Delaware Avenue bus which took you to the front door of the Institute. What a country I am thinking to myself.

After registration, I stayed for a class and father left. My teachers were two ladies, mother and daughter by name Ryan. Mr. Thomas Ryan was the Erie County Sheriff and his wife and daughter volunteered at the Institute. So I was put in the beginners class and started all over with learning my ABC's. My problem was not being able to distinguish when one word ends and the next starts, it sounded to me like a machine gun spewing bullets. But those ads in the bus were driving me crazy and I was determined to decipher them.

So I started carrying two dictionaries with me: English-Polish and other English-Czech. I'll show you who is the boss. I was determined to find every word in the dictionaries, mark it down and when I was home, try to put the words in order so they will make sense.

In two weeks, I was able to understand every ad in the bus and could not wait until they replaced them with new ones. And slowly but surely, I started absorbing the English language. After two weeks, I got my green card as a permanent resident and could go to Canada. The very next weekend, I took the bus to Toronto, showed the taxi driver my brother's address and I was reunited with Pana my sister-in-law and my nieces. To Pana's amazement, I started chatting a few words of English with my nieces and she was mad that she cannot speak the language. It is so difficult.

However, coming back to Buffalo, at the USA border, I ran into a snag. The border officer boarded the bus and was checking everyone's documents. When he came to me, I handed him my green card. I strained my ears to hear clearly, and he asks me where in Canada was I, that much I understood and said Toronto. And he asks, Why? And the _why_, I didn't know, thinking it is _where_ and I again responded Toronto. He became agitated and was hollering _why_, _why, why_ and then it dawned on me and I responded, _brother, brother, brother_, imitating him. The passengers started laughing. He (the border official) started laughing at least show some sense of humor. I pointed to the date of my arrival in America on the green card, and he told the crowd that I am only 2 weeks in the country. I received a bunch of smiles and few "Welcome to America", mostly from the women.

Since I was not working yet, I started picking up some evening classes in English at East High School at Fillmore Avenue. I also started reading the newspapers, getting to know the makeup of the city, and the things started clicking together, in a completely different direction for the better.

One Saturday afternoon, I went to Andreef's Restaurant and nobody was there, but Mike from the Strumica Mafia, as they were affectionately called. He was driving some old model Chrysler and asked me if I wanted to go to Chestnut Ridge Park, which I didn't have any idea where it was located. So he drives, over the Skyway, gets off on Ridge Road in Lackawanna and we are driving through the most unkempt, deteriorating neighborhood you can imagine. Mike looks at me and says, "see even America has bad neighborhoods, what you say to that." If I am going to live in such a neighborhood, I would take the very first flight from Buffalo back to Poland.

I will be charitable when I describe the relationship between mother and father as bad. Mother held some grudges against him, for all their years of separation, having to endure wars, worrying about her family, abandoning the household property, and father not responding for months, and sometimes not sending any financial help and not showing any care about my sisters. She finally let all of her frustration go, and let him have it. She was not the submissive wife, taking orders from him anymore, like in the old country. The tough, calculated and brutally hard conditions she had to go through had toughened her, and made her that much stronger and outspoken. Father was not a bad man at all, he would give you the shirt off his back. He was very generous, but had no warmth in relations, was stubborn, would not accept any suggestions, and it was his way or no way. You could not get any compliment out of him as it was not in his vocabulary. And I don't mean complimenting me, but for my mother, my brothers, my sisters, my sister-in-law. He treated them like they don't know anything. My brother, Spiro, was one of the smartest and most logical people in the area, everybody knew him and he had helped almost everyone. So when I would see them bickering, I would step between them and try to calm them down.

My classes in English progressed smoothly, I started understanding more and more, and started conversing with my new friends. I also started recognizing who speaks well and who struggles. And that was giving me more incentive. But one of the best incentives to go to school was very tangible, it was my daily routine which I loved very much. Before I left the

157

bus on Delaware Avenue and North Street to walk to the Institute, (about a mile or so), I saw Howard Johnson's restaurant on the corner. So the next day, I took the bus all the way to the school and after school, I walked to North Street to check out the restaurant. On the wall they had displayed different colored labels with different names of ice cream. Thirty-eight different tastes of ice cream, what a crazy country. So I started sampling a different taste every day until I had tried all 38 flavors. Nobody is going to kick me out of this country.

I had advanced to the next class and was conversing much more fluently. Every day, I saw a bunch of happy students with school uniforms from the nearby school, Canisius. I asked Mrs. Ryan what kind of school it is. She replied, "Oh, it is a boys high school, private and the richest people send their boys there." "Do you have to be rich to go there, I asked"? "No, you have to be smart first, but costs lots of money. Why you are asking me anyway"? "Because when I get married and have sons, that's where they are going", I said to Mrs. Ryan. Here I am broke, with no job, and no income. And talk about nonexistent expensive initiative "marzsenie szcientej glowi" Polish people say in this situation, which means the dreams of a cut off head.

In the fall of 1962, I was at East High School taking classes and some bulletin started coming through the radio. The Cuban Crisis had erupted in full force and very scary predictions were uttered by the pundits. And I got really mad because I finally got out of the Russian domination and they keep following me even here.

Soon after I came to USA, I had gone to register with the draft board. After full day of interviews and medical checkups, we were supposed to get an answer about the status of eligibility. While being interviewed, an officer spoke to me few words of Greek, and asked me if I want to serve in Greece. Any place but Greece, please. So I don't know my status yet, and "them Ruskies" are causing trouble next door. I could not care about me, going into service, I might become general and settle some scores. The Pentagon is so big that the rumors were circulating, one captain went on assignment and by the time he finished, came out a one star general. And another rumor was that one lady went with their newborn to see her husband, and by the time she found the exit, the baby was already speaking. A little silly humor, but my worries were about the parents.

So when I went home, there is a letter from the draft board. A bad omen, I thought, opening the letter. But good news, "category 4 extended liability" the card said. My mother was very relieved, but father? He could not care less, at least that was how he acted, and that is what I mean by "lost generation" and not understanding the system. And it was not only him, many other people of his generation neglected their families in much worse ways. Some were remarried with local women and some would not accept their families coming USA. I was constantly assuring mother, that the situation would improve, stay away from my father's shadow and don't pick fights about politics, like belonging to MPO.

So finally the liquor license came; the lawyer completed the paperwork, father signed it, paid the price and, we started looking for an apartment near the bar. And where was the location of the bar? Yup, you are correct, right smack in the middle of the slum on Ridge Road in Lackawanna. I did not know what to do – cry or laugh with such a fate. But the common sense and my pride prevailed and I accepted the challenge. I found fairly decent apartment one block away, mother and I cleaned the place; the floors, windows, kitchen, etc. Father called the sales men and stocked the shelves with alcohol and beer. And in no time, Ladies and Gentlemen, the THEATRE GRILL is open for business!

Upon the opening, we had a pleasant commotion. The word spread around and many old customers from

Seneca Grille came, many customers from the neighborhood came and many new customers came (their curiosity prevailed). And father found himself in his element. He hired a couple of barmaids, started teaching me about serving prices, ordering, and everyday was more challenging than the previous. I started recognizing the customers by their names and drinking habits. But still I had plenty of free time and could hold another job. I did not have a car but, Bethlehem Steel was within walking distance. I had applied at Ford Plant but had not heard from them. In the neighborhood was a Polish bakery and I stopped to buy some baked goods. To my pleasure, the owners were directly from Poland and we started speaking in Polish. "We have not seen you before", they said. I replied, "Because we moved here not long ago, we run Theatre Grill. I am not too busy, I am looking for job." They asked about Ford and I told them I had not heard from them. Then they asked if I had applied at Bethlehem Steel and if I wanted to work there. When I replied that I would want to work there, they told me to wait there and the lady went to the back room.

Ten minutes later, a police car showed up at the front door and the Captain of Lackawanna Police came inside. He said, "So you want a job, eh"? "Yes Sir!", I answered. Then he says "Come with me" and he takes me to the police car and we go to the unemployment office building. It was a very ornate, elegant sort of French architecture building. The place was full of people and I mean full. Mostly blacks, here and there sprinkled with whites. What a waste of time, I think to myself, certainly I am in last place on the hire list. Within the huge room, in the corner was a small office built to process the hires. The captain approached the office door. "Stay here", he says in Polish and goes inside. In about 15 minutes a fellow opens the door and hollers my name. So I go inside. "You understand English?", he asks. "Yes, I do", I replied. He shows me some drawing of metal staircase machinery, etc., marked with yellow, red and green paint. "You understand the meaning of these colors?" "Yes, I reply, red means don't touch, yellow means hold the railing, green means public space." He inquires how long are you in the States and I replied, "8 months". Then he tells me, "Tomorrow, Thursday, you go for x-rays and Monday you start working at 7am. Sign here, here, and here, and we are all done."

Then the Captain took me back to the bakery and that was the first and last time I saw him. Holy Lackawanna, what the heck, in just the last 40 minutes what had transpired? I go to bakery for a loaf of bread and wind up getting a job through the most unusual circumstances. Am I hallucinating? Thanks to the Sparks, owners of the bakery, I have a job.

I headed back to the Grill. When I opened the door of the business, the phone is ringing and father told me to take the call. I picked up the phone and the voice on the other side inquires if I am George. "Yes"? "Hi, this is Ford Company, you applied for a job and I want to know when you can start". I replied "Hold it second". I told my father it was Ford, and they want me to work for them. And father said that the policeman came as a favor for Sparks, took you there in person and now it would not look good to embarrass him. So I turned down Ford and started with Bethlehem Steel. The pay at that time was more or less the same level between both companies.

On Monday morning, I reported for duty. The foreman was of Polish decent, understood little Polish, and helped me a lot. He gave me a huge push broom, a wheelbarrow, and put me to work cleaning the tresses of the coal being dumped for the furnaces. There I saw another Macedonian, I had met before, Peter. So for couple of days, we kept sweeping and then the foremen put me inside at the furnace where the steel was boiling. I had to open the doors and throw various additives into the steel according to the order. After the first week, they changed my schedule to the afternoon shift and the following week to the night shift. It was a brutal trauma to my system, not only the shift work, but also the safety clothing you had to wear when the ovens were tapped to empty the steel. Thankfully, after a month, they put me on day shift at the splice bar. It was department where they were making parts to splice the rails together. It was a promotion or demotion, I did not know and didn't care, but the job was much cleaner and easier and the pay was the same.

So every morning I received a written order to assemble a certain number of pieces on wooden pallets, tie them with steel band, put the work # on and wait for the trucks to pick them up. When the truck arrived, I hooked up them with the chains and the crane operator puts them on the truck. Some days I had 3 orders, some days 10 orders. And between the hookups, I collected orders and money to go to the cafeteria to buy coffee and sandwiches for the guys. I did not like that assignment, but it was imposed by the foreman to keep the workers on the job. But the men were spoiled Americans. They ordered Coffees: black-black, sugar only-sugar and milk-milk only- double, double-double milk, double sugar. Milk and sugar, no coffee. Oops, Sandwiches: tuna, melt, ham and cheese, roast beef, BLT. Breads: Rye, wheat, white, toasted, Italian. But the worst thing I had to face was inside the tiny counter in the café. There were several women who looked like they overindulged on their lunches, and because they had to struggle to keep up with the orders without the benefit of air conditioning, their faces and hands were sweaty – They were also pushy like hell. Wait a minute, they don't understand me because I cannot pronounce the orders correctly. At this point, I had only been in the country for nine months.

So one day I talked to the foreman about my problem. He was an elderly fella and very fair. "George, he said "you are spoiling them bastards, you think that they get such a service home? Count how many coffees, how many sandwiches, make them all the same. When they are freezing their asses out on the line, you think they care what they are drinking or eating? And I see you struggle to give them the exact change. Round that to the next dollar and that's it". He said that he would tell them about it, so, they know what is going to happen.

So you can improvise here. What a great country, this America. So the new system started working for me beautifully, the women in the cafeteria started looking skinnier and when I was done with the orders, I would have in my pocket 3-6 dollars – a tip!

I worked 18 weeks in Bethlehem and they laid me off. When I worked at the plant, I would be at Theater Grill at 5 o'clock in the morning to clean the bar & floors, put the empties in boxes and in the storage, fill all the refrigerators with beer and the shelve with wine and alcohol, plus fix the cash register. All of this in 2 hours and, then at 7 o'clock, start my job at Bethlehem Steel. Father would come in at 10 o'clock in the morning, stay there until noon, and when the barmaid came in, he would go home. Then at 3:15pm, I would come from the factory, stay in the business until 9-10 o'clock at night, then father would come back and stay until closing.

We had a regular group of customers from Bethlehem, specially from the rigging department. Very hard workers, most of them veterans from the second world war, and very passionate drinkers. Once of them was George Kaczewich, a longtime friend of my father, but much younger. The next was Martin Winter from Ireland, and everybody called him Irish. George's nickname was Cookie and everybody called by the nickname. Then we had Giggy with permanent smile on his face, and a very unusual good character, Frank Morse. Then there was a quiet man usually Steve Book and last but not least, Steve Banko. I don't remember if Banko was a veteran but his son, Steve Banko served in the Vietnam War and was one of the most decorated heroes in the nation. To those people I owe gratitude because they made my life easier, not being only customers, but friends, and from them, I learned a lot about America. They were independent thinkers and the fiercest patriots. Frank and Giggy

166

taught me the rules of football. They were devoted to the Bills forever, and if I wanted to make them angry, all I had to say was the Bills stink and Frank would say with emphasis: "I got news for you, if don't like it, you can go back where you come from and play soccer!"

And then there was the "diva" of Theatre Grill, a short, stocky Hungarian known to all by the name of Lina. She was a good character, but a burned out alcoholic, and she could represent the USA at the Olympics in swearing if there had ever been such a game. She could swear in 5-6 languages and could put any sailor to shame. She and Cookie always had an argument going on about something trivial.

We had huge windows on the front of the bar and I could always see her coming from across the street. Her standard drink was glass of beer and shot of crème de mint. Before she came in, I had the drinks ready at her favorite spot and warned Cookie. And as soon as she opened the door, Cookie will start singing "Here she is Miss America" and Lina would answer, "Pocalaj my royal dupa." And it was stupid, but hilarious, the life of bar people.

I got a job on South Park Avenue, way down before Blasdell. I took the bus from the front of the bar at Ridge Road up to South Park and, I had to walk one mile to the factory. They were assembling aluminum doors and windows. Second shift was 3-11pm. A bunch of women were sitting and putting together (on a pneumatic table) various sizes of windows and, a few men were standing and assembling the doors on bigger tables. A black fella working on the morning shift explained to me how to put the frames on the table and fasten them with two screws on each end with an air gun. I started working and stocking the assembled doors on the wall and as soon as the clock reached 11 pm, I had to run the mile back to Ridge Road, so I won't miss the last bus at 12am. I survived the first day on the job and went there the next day. As soon I entered, the 3 owners, a father and 2 sons, started shaking my hand, slapping me on shoulders saying "good guy George, good guy".

As soon I enter the facility, the guy who broke me in yesterday runs away, without saying anything and most of the workers look at me with contempt. I was very puzzled thinking "what the hell I done"? The foreman, was also Polish and spoke a little bit of American-Polish, comes to me and asks me, "How many doors you assembled yesterday?" I replied, "I don't know, was I supposed to count them?" "*You assembled 128 doors the very first day. And the other guys assemble on average 60 doors. The record is 88 doors. So you done 40 doors better than the record and everybody is pissed at you because the management will demand bigger output from everybody and they are not as young as you are."* Honestly, I did not put any extra effort to raise the output, I was working at reasonable speed and I took all the coffee breaks with rest of them. But I immediately understood the implications and the sticky nuances of the free enterprise, as I recalled being preached at in Czechoslovakia about strikes, about speeding the assembly lines, about poor working conditions, about clashes between bosses and labor. And now, one misinformed worker: that's me, could start a fire between ownership and the other workers. I apologized to the foreman, asked him to explain to workers that, "I did not know, this won't happen again, but gradually in 3-4 days I will come down in production." Boy, this America is a strange country.

So the following day, I dropped to about 110 doors, and then below 100 and then the panic button rang in the Management office. In the interest of self-perseveration, they summoned me to the office and started sort of interrogating me as to why; who told me to cut production so far.

At Bethlehem, they paid $2.65 per hour, here they paid $1.25 per hour. So I assured them that nobody talked me about it or complained to me, simply that I was tired and had to run one mile after work to catch the bus. And with only $1.25 an hour, I can't afford to buy bicycle, much less a car. They promised me an increase in pay, and the following paycheck I sure got an increase, five cents per hour.

Since I did not have enough weeks to qualify for unemployment (you learn these rules fast), the next morning I went to the employment office at Bethlehem and gave them little bit of attitude for letting me go. They asked, "You want to work George?" Silly question, "sure I want to work." They told me to report to the storage beds department on Monday morning. Being in the office, who did I meet there? Stoyan Boshnakov, the "Strumica Mafia" chief. I did not know that he worked in Bethlehem, and was unemployed, that made me feel better, but I did not see him on the job at all, since he worked in different department and Bethlehem employed about 24 thousand people. So my assembler carrier career ended after two weeks and, I bet my record still stands.

But the storage yard job was something else again. Three shifts and the night shift was a killer for me. It messed up my metabolism, I could not sleep, eat or function properly. Wintertime on the shores of Lake Erie, working outside, piling the steel bars on top of each other per order, while the wind is blowing numbs you from cold. We had huge salamander burning wood chips and frequently went to warm ourselves up, but on front of you, you are burning and on back you are freezing.

Father reached age 65 and I filed the paperwork for social security. The money I was making on the jobs were going to the bank so I could buy a car and have some savings of my own, so I can regain my dignity. I went to the motor vehicle office. They gave me a small booklet with the rules of traffic, and told me to read it, and when you think you are ready, come back for the test. So I sat on the bench in the lobby, read the book and went back for the test. They give you only a learner's permit, you can't drive alone. But, I passed the test and I now had my learner's permit.

Cookie had an old Dodge. And he was my "teacher-instructor." I am sure I gave him ulcers, but he was nervous to begin with. One evening I was driving and he wanted to go to Lakeview to some bar to see his friend. The parking lot was full, so I looked for empty spot and tried to slow, down but, the brakes did not work. Cookie was hollering at me, "pump them, pump them, you stupid Greek". But it was too late, yes, I stopped by hitting another car. Cookie is all in panic, wants to take the steering wheel from me, but I did not give up. That's the only way to learn to drive, under pressure. He said "Back up" so I did. We came out of the car to see if there was any damage, but it was dark outside, and nobody saw us, so we got back in the car and left. Sorry fella for the damage, whoever you are, but I was young and stupid in those times. Cookie is threatening me that I will pay for his damage, but on that old jalopy, any dent could only improve the looks. Then he calms us both down as we approach our bar and assures me that he won't tell father about the mishap. "Tell him Cookie, I don't care!", I reply.

On a few Saturdays after closing the Theater Bar, Cookie would go home with his wife, Mary, and I would use his Dodge to take the Skyway to downtown. On Sunday morning, the city streets used to be empty, and I would drive all over Buffalo to familiarize myself with the city. I would look for all the stop signals, one way streets, warning signs, speed signs, street lights and whatever else. Father bragged to the customers that I made the appointment for the test drive. Manuel, one of the gang challenged me, that I would not pass the test. So the bet was made, that if I fail the driving test, everybody at the bar gets drink on me and if I make it, Manuel will buy everybody a drink. I took the test and I was sure that I passed. "You will get the result in the mail in about a week", the instructor said and let me go. Obviously Cookie and his Dodge were with me. "How did you do?", Cookie asks. I don't know now, in a week I will know.

So next week on Wednesday, I go into the bar to replace father and he hands me a letter from the motor vehicle office. He is curious to know and when I told him that I passed the test, he was very happy and says he will make sure Manuel buys the drinks tonight. I said. "No father, not tonight, Wednesday is not a busy night. Friday when I come in at evening, give me the letter and I will pretend I just got it". So Friday, we opened the letter, of which we knew the outcome, and Manuel got stuck with a big tab. Father was not driving because years back in Virginia, he worked as a delivery man for a big bakery and on one of his trips he ran over a pig and would not drive again.

In the spring of 1963, I was ready to have a car and started looking around. I found a neat small car which would later turn out to be the linchpin of Ralph Nader's narratives; the Chevy Corvaire. It was a little bit tight for father, but in the back seat, he had plenty of space by himself. Not knowing anything about cars, I called my brother from Toronto, and the next day he came. "For this price, it is in excellent shape", he says. He told me to talk the dealer into dropping a few bucks from the price and to change the front tires. And the next day, I told the world, "if you do not like the way I drive, stay away from the sidewalks!" It was proper to give the people fair warning. Well, obviously the dynamics of our lifestyle changed. No more waiting for busses. I started taking mother to stores for shopping, which it opened new horizons for her.as well. I started driving to Toronto to visit my brother Spiro and to

Cleveland to see my sister Vasilka and I could have any job wherever.

In the meantime, at the bar, Irish still drank his Carling beer, Cookie anything and, Frank Morse – Cooks Ale, made nearby at Dunkirk, NY. In all the time we had the business, nobody, but nobody else asked for one bottle of Cooks Ale, except Frank. Six cases a week, like clockwork. Lina was still bilingual swearing and Mr. Green, a black fellow who owned the nearby car wash, "liked his coffee like his women, black and hot" as he often was telling me.

We started getting plenty of Arabian customers originally from Yemen. Cookie knew many of them and they were always teasing and joking. He was particularly close with Mohamed Hussain but everybody called him Bobby. But not Cookie, when Bobby came in, he always ordered a drink for Cookie, but Cookie would always say, "No, I don't drink with Camel Jockeys." And when Cookie ordered for Bobby, he would say, "No I don't drink with stupid Polocks." We had so many bizarre characters, that it will take a book on its own to describe them.

I was having a drink at Andreef's in downtown Buffalo, when Radko came and sat next to me. I bought him a drink and Tom, the owner, came over. Radko asks him if he would cash his payroll check. He replied "Sure, sign it." And Radko put his check at

174

front of me. I could not avoid reading it - $146 net. I asked, "Radko, how many hours of work does this check represent? What do you mean? 40 hours. What type of work you are doing?" He told me he was a painter. Since I had never heard the word painter before, I had to ask the word painter meant. And, he tells me in Macedonian. Right on the spot my future changed and I became a painter too. Radko said, "But you have the bar." "Not for long, since my father retired", I countered. The reason was that at Bethlehem working three shifts, outside under any weather conditions, my take home pay was $72, and the painter was taking home double for 40 hours. The next day, Radko tells me that Monday I can start painting. And my career as a steelworker is also ended. Darn it, this the second career finished.

The Irishman's (Martin Winter) wife worked at the Loblaw's food chain as an assistant manager. They had three boys. One day, Irish gives me a coupon, and says, "go to Loblaws and every time you buy, they punch some holes on the ticket and when you finish, they peel something off and there is an amount revealed. Whatever money is there, it is yours, my family cannot participate in that." So I am in America, I have a car, and I can shop to my content. So after the umpteenth trip to the store, the cashier punched the last hole on the ticket. Nobody was behind me in line,

175

but in front of me was a fat, elderly woman clearing her groceries. And the cashier screams "We have a winner" and activates a loud buzzer. The woman in front of me turns toward me, hugs me and plants a huge, sweaty kiss right in my mouth. *Gross.* The manager comes and congratulates me and many people were excited for about 10 minutes. I was the moments hero without earning it. The prize was one thousand dollars. I had to go the following week to get the check. And, they took bunch of pictures of me for advertising purposes. But after that woman kissed me, I went home with all the windows open, kept spitting all the way home, and came close to vomiting. Her sweat was salty.

The next week I offered the money to Irish. It was his doing that I got the winning ticket. But no way would he take it; his wife had 3 tickets to give away to anybody that she liked. One was for $300, one for $500 and one for $1000, without knowing which ticket is worth what amount. So the "social secretary" of the Theatre Grill, Lina, kept reminding me to have a cake for Irish because in three days it was his birthday. And at his birthday, among the cake and drinks, I slipped Irish $500 in an envelope with note written on the envelope: DON'T OPEN TILL TOMORROW MORNING. But, he spent most of the money at the bar anyway.

Chapter VII   New Friends and Family

And then I started my painting career. I hooked up with Radko for a couple of months and then I got laid off. The contractor he worked for was bidding on the jobs and when the project was finished, if he doesn't have another job for you, you got laid off and waited until next job. Blagoj worked in Niagara Falls for the Commercial Painting Company. He was working there a long time and assured me there was plenty of work. So I started there and worked for Mr. Spiro Manos, an elderly gentleman who treated me supremely. Every winter for about 3-4 months, we were off the work due to the nature of work, and Western New York's wonderful winters. But it was a union job and pay scale, and we collected unemployment and supplemental union benefits, which we had contributed to. So the money was pretty good.

I took Stoyan as a guest to the annual dance at the International Institute. There were students and faculty members from all over the world. Attending classes with me were a mother and beautiful daughter from Cuba. And I introduced Stoyan to the daughter, Miriam was her name. And they started dating and eventually got married. Before the marriage, a civil ceremony in city hall, Stoyan calls me and asks me to go with him to look for apartment. The "Strumica

Mafia" lived in a apartment on Elmwood Avenue and since they seldom stayed home, one apartment was good enough for 16 people. Stoyan had some ads indicating apartments for rent on Delaware Avenue (for those times it was ritzy neighborhood). We rang the bell and voice came through the outside speaker: "Yes, what you want?" Stoyan tells him about the ad and asks to see the apartment. "Where are you from?" the voice asks. Buffalo Stoyan says. "No originally, what country are you from?", the voice asked. "Yugoslavia", Stoyan replies. "We don't want Yugoslavian", and click the conversation is over. "I don't want you also, you bastard", Stoyan answered. But, I don't know if the "bastard" hear him. Eventually they rented beautiful second floor apartment on Richmond Avenue. Then "little" George got married and also rented an apartment on Richmond. They called him little because of his height, which was considerably shorter than his brother Blagoj.

One evening I went to the White Eagles Polish Singing Society Headquarters on Broadway, where they had a dance. In the course of drinking and observing people, I noticed two girls together, sort of lost in the place and I started a conversation. Hi-by-this or that, I don't remember the buzz word of that era, but I started dancing with one of them, who was not only beautiful but also had beautiful black hair. So we made a date, and another and another, and soon we were seeing each other every opportunity we had. I met her parents, a working family from the Lovejoy section. And every time I am with her, I feel more and more comfortable, not pretentious. She worked for the electric company and her name was Bette. As a matter of fact, her name is still Bette. Our relationship grew to the point that I knew I would propose to her, but I did not like the circumstances I was in with the business. I could never have a family and be in bar business, and father was slipping sideways; he started looking for consolation in the bottle. Bobby Hussain had asked me several times to sell him the business, but I did not take him seriously. I was doing well with my painting job, so I did not need the burden of caring for a business and putting up with people like Lina.

In 1967, I completed 5 years in USA and applied for citizenship. And I went out of my way to learn the laws of the American government system. After some time, they called me to the federal building with a sponsor for the civil examination. And the sponsor was obviously Cookie. We went to the office of the examiner, he asked Cookie how long he knows me and if I will make a good citizen, some obvious questions and then turns to me. "Do you know how to read English?" I replied "Yes!" So he gave me a book to read a few sentences. He asked "Do you know how to write?" Again I replied, "Yes!" So he gave me a pencil and told me to write the sentence: Today is a good day – and I wrote that. And the next question: "How about American history?" I respond, "How about you ask me." And I am braced myself, I wanted to concentrate. So he asked "Who was the first American president?" And I lost it. I jumped up from the chair, broke the pencil in half and threw it on his table, and with very agitated voice, told him, "Come on, I've known the answer to this question since I was four, ask me something with substance!" He looks at me startled, somehow with my reaction and tells me that we Europeans know the American history better than the Americans. "Sign here", he say, "and you will be notified." Cookie was also surprised too with my reaction, and asked the officer if I passed, to make sure. He said to Cookie that it is his fault for asking such a lame question, but he liked my answer and thought I would make a terrific citizen. Being reassured with his statement, Cookie and I left the building faster than fast. But I should have known it going back to bar, Cookie embellished my reaction so much, that it sounded like I almost attacked the poor person and we almost were arrested. That was Cookie.

About a month later, I was sworn in at the federal building by a federal judge to the American citizenship and I will proudly keep this honor as long as I am alive. After the swearing-in ceremony, the Daughters of the American Revolution were serving donuts and soft drinks to about 40 of us newly minted American citizens. I cannot put in words the overwhelming feeling I experienced after becoming an American citizen. I saw myself traveling all over the world with an American passport, and it gave me tremendous reassurance that I would not be ignored and stepped on over my birthplace. I would not have to travel under imposed conditions to various countries, not having roots of my own and I would not be at the mercy of the next unforeseen forthcoming regime which did not appeal to me and would have a devastating effect on my psyche. This move completely eliminated those possibilities and restored my balance and worthiness within me. And made me very proud to be in position to benefit from the brilliance and wisdom of the great minds who formed the Constitution and wrote the laws of conduct of this country. The great builders who transformed and developed this country to its current magnificence and the great soldiers who fought and gave the supreme sacrifice so we little people in the context of this all, can live a full and dignified life.

One Friday night at the bar, an accident happened. Stanley, a steady drunkard, came out of the bathroom with blood is squirting all over like he had slaughtered a pig. He had stumbled and fallen on top of a radiator. Cookie was there and I told him to close the bar if I am not back by the time it wrapped up. We covered Stanley with a towel and rushed him to Our Lady of Victory hospital. By the time they finished with him, it was 3 am, and the bars closed at 2 am.

Stanley got about 30 stitches to close the bleeding and would not agree to stay overnight so I had to take him home. I was a total wreck worrying and I was sure he is not going to make it. All night I could not sleep, thinking about Stanley, and Saturday morning I headed to the bar to tell father what had transpired. It was too early, as it was only 9:30 am and there was only one customer at the end of the bar. Father comes from the kitchen and seeing me, scolds me, asking why I am here so early on a Saturday. The moment I started telling father, the customer at the corner looks at me and smiles. Yes, I was ready to kill the SOB, but how can you kill a person twice, since I was sure Stanley would die overnight! Yes, it was Stanley. I told father what transpired and I got hold of Bobby Hussain. "Bobby", I said, "this is George. How much money did I ask you to give me for the business? $14,000 and how much did you offer? Ten thousand. Bobby, let's split it to $12 thousand. At the closing you will give me $10 thousand dollars and I will give you one year to pay the remaining two thousand." Bobby countered, "A year and a half, George, OK?" Ok, Bobby", I said "for you only. On Monday call your lawyer." Tough bargainers those camel jockeys. I told father we are getting out of here and are getting two thousand more than father expected and he was happy.

In the meantime, the relationship with Bette became more intense and in August of 1967, we got engaged. And then mother took over. Being the local seer, weather predictor, and medicine woman, (every family had on in the village), she insisted that we get married the same year, 1967, because the next year is a leap year and was not going to be lucky year. So we hurried the arrangements, rented an apartment on Fernald Avenue in Lackawanna. In November of 1967, we had a very lovely wedding with our families and friends.

A few months later, the Theatre Grill was out of my system. Bette was taking the bus to work and I worked in Niagara Falls. It was an industrial type of painting, mostly sandblasting, spraying factories, water tanks, and dust collectors. But we (now we are two) had to take some drastic steps to improve our lot. Winter was coming and that was the time I usually got laid off. Every contractor wants the best worker, and I established myself with great reputation as being reliable, fast and a hard worker, so most of the contractors begged me to work for them. But I was loyal and stuck with Mr. Manos. Most of the contractors were Greeks and speaking the language was extra bonus for me. My wife and I agreed that her paycheck would never come home, that is, as soon she got paid, the check went straight into the bank. That winter, three of us subcontracted several buildings from another contractor who had won the job from the Buffalo Housing Authority. As I was learning more and more of the inner workings of the NY State, I noticed that those authorities are like mushrooms, growing all over the state and behaving like kingdoms with their staff, their own police, etc. So to paint a one bedroom apartment, we were getting $45, a 2 bedroom $55, in cash. It was a harrowing job as the apartments were occupied and often smelled of all sorts of cooking and some of them were in a deplorable state of cleanliness, but hey, all the cash was green and that's what counted. So each of us tried to finish an apartment a day and, on Fridays, we were meeting the boss in Kenmore at some Bulgarian bar, giving him the number of units we had finished and getting paid.

So collecting unemployment and sub pay from the union, and making extra cash, we were very comfortable and did not miss my wife's check at all. The next spring I started working in Niagara Falls and, as usual, planned to work there until December. One week we had plenty of maintenance painting at the abrasive making factory, Union Carbide. We were painting a bunch of dust collectors on concrete bases, with very little clearing space on the edge of the concrete. The one I was working on was situated almost next to the chain link fence and on top of the post was a round ball for decorative purposes. My left hand was stuck above the metal frame and I held the bucket in the other hand without being able to see the paint. I would blindly dip the brush in the bucket and paint the metal. In order to balance myself better, I stepped on top of the decorative ball on the post. The damaged ball was rotten and broke, I lost my balance and dropped a bucket full of gray oil paint on top of my head. I was all covered with dripping paint, my eyes are shot and burning, I can't see. Thankfully, somebody saw me, and ran to get help. Someone helped me to the ground and somebody else brought rags, and I wiped myself off. Then we headed to the truck where we had 50 gallon drum full with paint thinner. I turned the spigot on and washed my head, face, and neck, with paint thinner. The thinner burned the skin, on my neck and face and I was in agony. I always carried extra clothing in my car, so I grabbed them went to the showers and after long time washing in cold water, I finally started feeling some relief.

That factory was not conducive to for my health because the very next day I jumped backward on the ground from the base of the collector and did not make anything of that. But, about ten minutes later, my foot started sliding in the shoe and when I removed it, my sock and shoe were full of blood. What happened? I retraced my steps back to the place where I jumped and sure enough there was a two foot long piece of 2x4 with a nail sticking up. I rushed to the nursing station where the nurse washed and disinfected the foot, bandaged it and sent me to the hospital for a tetanus shot. I left the factory and on the way home, I stopped at Columbus Hospital on Niagara Street where they stuck me with tetanus shot. The next morning I asked the boss to send me to a different job, which he obliged. Well, every job has some drawbacks, some militaristically put, have collateral damage.

The town of Cheektowaga, between French, Losson and Transit Roads was drastically expanding and one Saturday Bette and I went to look at some models. I had spent enough time on construction sites in Poland, but they were Spartan buildings, brick and mortar buildings for workers with just the basic necessities, like water, heat, plumbing, the aesthetics were secondary. But here we saw single houses or duplexes finished to perfection, no exposed plumbing pipes, no electrical wires showing on outside walls, choice of flooring, cabinets and appliances, your head started turning around. After assessing our situation, we decided to build a two family house.

One particular builder, Joe Gialanza, had the best designs and we made an appointment to see him and see what can he do for us. Besides Joe, there was another gentleman, Floyd Garfield, who was handling all the technical aspects, e.g., materials, pricing of the operation. We picked a nice corner lot, chose a two family model, and after few more meetings with Floyd, the deal was sealed. We would have 3 bedrooms, a kitchen, a big bathroom, a huge family room on each floor, a 2 car garage, a patio, a back yard, and huge basement, the whole works for $31 thousand. And since I was going to paint it myself I squeezed Floyd on a couple of thousand, so the price came down to $27 thousand. We put down $12K and took mortgage for $15K.

But Floyd was not merely a construction guy, he in many was a wizard in what he was doing. No machines, no calculators, pen and yellow legal pads only, he would specify every piece of lumber, every nail, every measurement, everything, why and why not, the code laws, the zoning requirements and on top of that he was a perfect gentleman.

From the beginning, we kept it quiet from my parents with the idea that if anything went wrong, we would not disappoint them. Every morning, Bette took the bus for work and I would come from Niagara Falls through the city, pick her up and we would go home. From the moment they started raising the house, we would swing over and to see the progress. When the roof was on and you could see the layout, we went to pick my parents and show them the house. We showed them the lower floor, then went upstairs, these are the bedrooms, this is the kitchen and so on. "Wait a minute", father asked, "why do you need 2 kitchens, 2 family rooms, etc?" This upper one is for us, and the lower is for you. And then it dawned on them, and father started crying, for maybe the second time in his life, and mother started scolding me, questioning why we kept it for so long from them, and why, after being married for two and a half years, we are proud owners of a beautiful duplex and for the very first time in our lives, I was living together with my parents in our own house. The checks Bette was stashing in the bank produced results. What a country, only in America.

Stoyan and Miriam were also looking for a house, preferably in a neighborhood where they do want Yugoslavians and, we introduced them to Joe and Floyd, and they started negotiating for a house in a new development about a mile away from us and eventually they bought a split level model. So now we are close neighbors. But in meantime they had a beautiful girl named Maritza, named after Stoyan's mother (who had died young) and Stoyan always missed her terribly, being denied the longer relationship between mother and son. In those times and past, most of the Macedonian community saved and owned their houses, but not having better command of the language and having a desire to stick close to each other, usually were buying older existing homes. Also, they were not being able to navigate through the system of contracts, blue prints, realtors, lawyers, zoning and building codes. To many these were incomprehensible obstacles, and they were suspicious. So ignorance is not always a bliss. So Stoyan and I were first among our generation to move to a brand new home.

That past winter, Blagoj, George and I worked at the Kenfield Projects and the temperature in the empty apartment was so high, the paint was sliding from the walls. So we opened all the windows and out of frustration or happiness, started signing Macedonian songs. Not one of us was able to carry a tune. We did not only sing the songs, but actually kill them! I was working close to the open window and upon sticking out my head to gulp a fresh air, some lady seeing me, screamed, "Hey Sinatra" Taking this as a compliment, I answered "Yes, what?" and she responds loudly: "Shut up!" And then apologizing says, "I worked all night and can't get any sleep! Please." And I said, "OK, but this is the last free concert, next time we will charge you." "No," she said, "I will pay you not to sing." So our careers as singers was over. But I am sure that we chased all the mice from the building.

By March, the famous Buffalo snows started subsiding and we were called back to work. A row of chemical factories, next to the Niagara River, separated by Robert Moses Parkway, were waiting for us for a coat of fresh paint. The work itself I could handle, but the stinky smell each factory was emitting was intolerable. Each factory was producing different products and every product has its own distinctive smell, and they clashed and made you dizzy. One hot day, a painter was assigned to paint the metal around the huge air conditioner on top of the roof. After few hours of work, the asphalt started melting from the hot sun and his boots got stuck in the goo. We did not see him coming down for lunch and from the ground he was invisible and with all the noises and humming from the machinery, you could not even hear the poor guy. Late that afternoon, the foreman had the presence of mind to climb up the ladder to check and there he is stuck in the roof up to his ankles, not being able to free himself. So they called the fire department and the fireman climbed up next to him with a huge hook, cut his shoelaces, tied him on and lifted him up, the shoes, maybe they are still there, on the roof.

We had a co-worker, a nice Italian kid who always was mooching something from everybody. Be it cigarette or candy, or chewing gum, part of lunch, or coffee, he was always was asking to share it. One day Kiro brought for lunch, a bunch of boiled eggs. And as soon as he saw it (Peter was his name), he asked Kiro for an egg. Kiro gave it to him conditionally. You have to crack it like I will. Well how? This way, and Kiro smashed the egg over his head. So Peter does the same thing but Peter's egg was raw and he literally wound up with egg on his face.

At that time, my father had some constipation problems and the doctor prescribed him some white tablets to chew in the evening and they helped him. Those tablets resembled exactly the chewing gum, Chiclets. So Kiro fixed Peter with the egg, but knowing him, he would still beg for items. The next morning the boss dispatched us four guys to Lewiston to paint a water tower. I, Peter, a black man, (an excellent worker named Ray who I always enjoyed working with) and the boss's favorite, another George. Before our destination, I opened the container, told George in

Greek what's happening, swallowed 2 real Chiclets. Before I closed my mouth, Peter extended his hand saying, "May I have a Chiclet, George?" "Sure Pete", they are the last two, have them." At the site, we emptied the truck, George and I went to the top of the tank, about 100 feet high, and using ropes, Peter and Ray hooked on the tools and paint, and we would raise them up. Then Pete comes up. On one side of the support leg for the tank, there were metal steps welded. Ray started climbing up. Peter was showing signs of stomach distress and started desperately going down to the bathroom. He could not hold it and let it go and everything falls on Ray's head, and Ray does not know what happened and hollers to us, "come down you guys, it is raining." And then he sees Peter speeding down and Ray reverses the direction downward, while screaming at Peter; "you stupid dago, you shit on top of me." The tank belongs to a military base, and there were still some buildings left with operating plumbing so they went for the showers. But the day was ruined, and we did not do much work. George and I were laughing and Peter and Ray were arguing. Do you think Peter stopped mooching? No way.

First, I had started associating with bunch of Polish teams, where we played and organized volleyball and soccer teams and travelled between

Western NY and Canada, where other Polish teams were situated. Being Europeans, obviously we played soccer and we started a Macedonian team – the Balkans. Members were Italian, Polish, German, and Greeks, and we all belonged to the same league and travelled to different cities to compete. I don't have to tell you that the game is physical because you know it, but I will tell you anyway. Many unintended collisions turned out to be very intended and many times bloodletting was the result. We had a halfback, Cvetko Fotevski, when he started chasing the ball, he became a runaway locomotive and whoever he collided with, that "whoever" always paid the price being flattened on the field. Another member, Boris was a menace to the goalkeepers, he could score from any angle. We were playing the Halia Club in South Park on the Buffalo-Lackawanna border. We started the game shorthanded because Akim was late. We always had substantial crowds. Our wives, girlfriends and other soccer fans on both teams came and this game being played close to the residential area had more than the usual crowd. The game was going on and here comes Akim, and undressing on the run, joins the team. He did not have the on regulation shorts, because he did not want to waste time, so he played with his boxers on. Well the boxers had the typical slit on the front and Simka, the wife of Tom from Andreff's restaurant, hollers at him, "Akim, stuff it, stuff it in." And Akim, in all of his glory, turns toward the crowd and responds, "How can I stuff it, since nobody passed me the ball." Obviously, he was thinking about scoring a goal. Then he realized that the stuff it was meant for his genitals being exposed. From the beginning, Stoyan and I struck a long genuine friendship, but as the time progressed, we became very good friends also with Akim and Cvetko.

At our home, my parents enjoyed (for the first time), a normal relaxed family life. Mother used to go with Bette to the store and buy their type of foods and make Macedonian dishes to their heart's content. My mother would work in the garden while father sat on the patio and read his Bulgarian propaganda. He started once lecturing me about politics and I cut him short. Father, the politics brought us nothing but misery and a disruptive family life. I will buy you a subscription to your Nova Makedonia paper as long as you are alive but I don't believe in this. I am very interested in American politics and don't want to hear anything about the stinking Europeans. And it worked, he never tried to indoctrinate me into his politics again.

But I wanted to know about his life in USA. And he used to tell me stories from different cities he worked in. In St. Louis, he belonged to "the gang" (a group of friends who knew each other from the village) and they used to look for jobs in small groups. And, in St. Louis, they washed their clothes on the banks of Mississippi River. In Detroit, they slept two people in one bed to save money. One guy worked and the other slept. In Buffalo, he worked at a bakery and every day on his way home, the son of the owner used to give him a loaf of fresh bread, but one day his father was in and when the son handed him the bread, the father smacked it from his arm and instead gave him old loaf. My father was insulted and left them. And because of that, he went to Virginia where started delivering bread for some bakery. That is where he ran over a pig and after that time, he never drove again. After some time, he came back to Buffalo and got a job at Bethlehem Steel for $0.37 per hour. He was telling me many stories of hardships that are too painful to repeat. Immigrants were associating by the villages they came from. People from Nivici used to go to the red brick bank, people from Grazdeno to the white building and that is how they were describing the banks they dealt with, not by the real names such as Marine Midland Bank or Manufacturers and Traders Trust Company.

When we had Theatre Grill, there was a clothing store called Watsons. When father needed to buy something I was going to take him to Watsons. "No, no, not there", he emphatically refused. So I asked, "Why not there?" He tells me that in the1930's, a few of my friends were wearing some nice hats, but I was embarrassed to ask them where they bought them. So I went to Watson's and told the owner what I needed. He gave me all sorts of hats but not the one I was looking for. And when I said no, this one is wrong, he said no the hat is not wrong, you head is wrong. I turned around and delivered a punch right in his face, and he flew in the air and landed on top of a rack of clothing. Two sales girls started screaming, one was going to call the police, but the owner got up, and stopped her from calling the police. He shook my hand, apologized and gave me the hat for free. I threw the hat back and left. So that was my father. I took him to different store.

In August of 1970, we had our first child and we named him Gregory. I think that event extended my parents life by about 10 years. Bette stopped working and having built-in nanny helped tremendously. Mother was hovering all over sometimes to the distraction and annoyance to Bette. And I had to tell her to lay off a little bit. I could not wait to come home and be with my son.

The following year, I completed a few private jobs where the money really helped, but I was doing that on the weekends, since I could not quit my regular job. Then Joe Gialanza called me and asked me who painted my house. When I told him that I did that, he was surprised to hear it and asked me if I wanted to paint his houses, since he needed new painter. Having a mortgage on a new home, a new baby, and a wife not working, plus the benefits of having steady union job, made it very difficult to make up my mind to let go of what I had and start new on my own. Plus, I was without any experience or financial backing. But the desire to be my own boss, to make a change for a better life and to face a challenge won over. The limited security, if it did not work, I could always get back.

So in March of 1972, ten years after I came to the United States, I established a private entity by the name of Colony Painting and Wall Covering. It sounded great, but sounding great and a buck will only buy you a cup of coffee. I went to see my boss, Mr. Manos, with a bottle of his favorite spirit, before he called me back to work. I told him that I appreciated all of the 6 years I had worked for him and that I am was not coming back. Initially he was taken aback and asked who stole me from him. After explaining him my intentions, his mood changed and he took me to his huge shop next to the office and said, "You see this equipment, it is all yours until you establish yourself.

197

Come and borrow it anytime, anything you need." I
did not expect such a generous offer from him and I
was flabbergasted with the offer, but assured him that
I would be doing residential painting only. And from
then on Colony Painting started beautifying America.

Joe did not have any houses ready for painting and
I was facing the prospect of being idle for a week or so.
And already I started doubting my decision, going out
on my own. But, somebody had recommended me and
a woman called me to paint part of her home's interior.
Two day's work plus the materials for $360. As I was
packing my tools in the used station wagon I had just
bought, she paid cash. Out of the house comes her 8
year old daughter, crying. I ask, "Why are you crying
sweetie?" Her reply was "Because I can't get my bike
until next week." After I asked her where her bike
was. she replied, "Down the street at the mechanic's
shop. So I took her hand and we went to the mechanic.
"What is the damage for the bike mister?", I asked.
"$37, he responds." I paid him the money, she got her
bike and by the time I reached my car, she already was
home and had told her mother what happened. The
mother comes out saying, "George, please, she could
have waited until next week and I will pay you back
next week." So I said, "Mrs. (she had a name, but sorry
I forgot it), you already paid me. So you do not owe me
anything." I have a younger son and know that kids

are attached to their bikes. She thanked me and hugged me and in next few days I got several calls from her relatives for painting.

Another fella called me from Cheektowaga to paint the exterior of his ranch house. The front doors only and the 3 sides of all wooden siding. Lots of scraping and sweating for $900. And I never saw him coming or going and did not know where he went. I got absolutely no feedback whatsoever. I left him a note on the front door that the following morning I would finish the job having only the front door and the garage frame left to complete (about one hour of work). The next day upon arriving, I noticed a fancy Cadillac on the street and the man's wife is putting some suitcases in the car. He asked how much time I had left to finish and I told him that I would be done within the half hour. We walked into the garage and he says that they have to go to Cleveland, so to please lock all the doors when I leave. I agree. "You know", he says, "I have been watching you all the time and see how hard you worked and beautiful job you have done. I have never seen person working so hard." How the heck he was watching me when I never saw him at all, I still cannot figure out. He asked, "Are you married George?" Of course, I replied "Yes". He pulled a wad of money from his pocket and counting all hundreds asked, "$900?" Again, I replied "Yes." "Here is one thousand", he said, "take your wife to dinner." And, he thanked me and left. And then I had no doubts about my move as I had made over $1300 for 7 days of work. What a country!

Then I started working on the new houses. Soon I realized that I needed help, because the two story houses required more muscle to move the scaffolding around. I also bought a new van which was ideal for storing the materials. And the jobs started coming from unexpected sources. Besides the new homes, I had callings for private homes, churches, supermarkets, bowling alleys, etc. As the time was progressing, I was acquiring more and more expertise, because besides the physical painting of the object, there were other nuances involved, pricing, buying, scheduling, communication with the clients and money managing. My crew grew to five workers and my wife got involved on the administrative side with the rules and regulations, accounting, insurances and other requirements from the silent partner, the 800 pound gorilla, otherwise known as our government. How come nobody informed me before? I thought you finished the job, got paid and go spent the monies. But New York is not called the Empire State for nothing. History teaches that all empires were built on blood and sweat of many civilizations and now I guess it is our turn, the sweat of New Yorkers. On Ellis Island, in a building that my father went through twice, there is a huge picture of Italian worker coming to America on a ship. Back home they were telling us the streets in America are paved with gold. But they did not tell us that we were going to be the ones paving them.

My sister, Vasilka, had come from Lorrain and picked up my parents for a few weeks to stay with her. She was doing it almost every summer and it was giving mother a chance to catch up with many other ladies in Lorrain who had come from Poland. The morning they left, I went to work. About 2pm, Bette comes to the job site and tells me that father had some medical setback and they took him to an Ashtabula hospital. I went home, changed and drove to Ashtabula. My sister was crying, so Alex, her husband explained to me what transpired. Because it was getting late, I told my sister to go home and I would stay and talk to the doctors. First I called Dr. Schultz at Millard Fillmore Hospital who was my parent's doctor. He told me to bring him to the emergency room there and that somebody will wait for him. Then I located the local doctor, who treated him, an elderly gentlemen, who with big concern explained father's situation. He told me that my father had cancer of the stomach and he had at the most six months to live. I decided not to tell my mother anything until Dr. Schultz examined him, but knowing from experience with mother, I doubted the prognosis. Both had a strong constitutions, with no colds, no flu, and although mother had developed hypochondria in Poland, I had taken her to at least 15 doctors, who did not find anything wrong physically. Dr. Schultz finally diagnosed her with anxiety and nervous stomach, prescribed her sedatives and her disposition improved dramatically. Every time she prayed, she would mention Dr. Schultz in prayers and wished him all health and long life.

When we finally arrived at Millard Fillmore Hospital, some young doctor came and took father inside and said to go home, because Dr. Schultz had admitted him and he would take all the tests overnight, so Dr. Schultz will have them tomorrow. By the time I got home, it was 2 o'clock in the morning. I had made a 12 hour trip between the hospitals. The next afternoon, after work, I went to see father in the hospital. He was in much better shape, stabilized, with IV in his veins. I asked for Dr. Schultz, and he took me to a conference room where he told me there was no evidence of cancer, whatsoever. He told me that father had a strong case of diabetes, and that they were going to hold him for about a week until his sugar level stabilized. Mother, after seeing him in Ashtabula and witnessing the whole episode, had him already dead and started selecting burial clothing for him. After I explained that there is no cancer, but he has diabetes, and will be okay, she started complaining "what kind of country is this with such a silly sickness, nobody had diabetes in the old country and everybody eats sugar." Well, you go and try to explain it to her because her reasoning did not jive with reality. Before father was discharged from the hospital, the staff trained me how to handle and inject insulin, and all of the sudden, I became a medic. Twice a day I'd prepare the proper dose and stick it in his skin. "Does not hurt you?", mother would ask me. "Why should it hurt me?, I responded, father gets the needle." Our neighbor, Janet was a nurse, and offered to do it, but I settled for her to do it only when I was not home.

Otherwise my parents enjoyed the house, the life, baby sitting for Gregory, he was the apple of their eyes, and they were aging gracefully. Mother was always a complainer. This is hurting me and that is hurting me or I could not sleep all night, but come dinner time, she would compensate for all the lost sleep with food. "Last night I died from pain", she would say and I would say " how did you die when you are talking to me?". "Don't you trust me?", she'd respond. And I would reply, "Mom I trust you that something is hurting you in the legs, but

I don't know anybody dying from pain in the legs. You know who is dying? All those doctors in Poland

who were examining you and you outlived them."
Father was the opposite. I don't remember him
complaining about anything, no matter how much it
hurt him. He complained only when his newspaper
would be late and when I would refuse him a drink
after the onset of his diabetes.   The very first
question to the doctor prior to discharge was, "Doctor,
can I have AN occasional drink?" "No" the doctor
sternly ordered him, "no alcohol at all." "What should I
drink?" father asked. The reply was "Water, Alex,
water." So father said, "Doctor, you know who drinks
water? Only the frogs drink water." So quietly the
Doctor told me he can have only a beer after a meal
and no more than one bottle a day.

And Colony Painting? I got much more than I
bargained for because after the third year of existence,
the volume tripled. And I employed around 15
employees or more, depending on the season. The
Vietnam fiasco was coming to the end and I was
resolved to the idea that I'll employ Vietnam Veterans
whenever they are available and most of the times I
had 2-3 veterans. Many guys on the crew were
Macedonians, and there was no nepotism involved at
all. They were hired and fired strictly on its merits.
    We were painting the personal house of Joe
Gialanza, an elegant estate in Elma, and one morning,

as soon as I entered his driveway, the owner, Joe, was pulling up with his Cadillac to leave. He stopped, exchanged few words and said he would be back at 12 o'clock. That was enough for prankster #1, Risto, who overheard the conversation. Before 12pm, he lowered the plank about 4 feet, called all four Macedonian painters to stay on that plank including him and compelled me to give him the signal when Joe entered the driveway. When I saw the Cadillac's front end and when Joe could see the front of his house, I said "Now", and all 5 of the guys jumped on the ground and acting like they were in a panic, spread left and right toward the trees. "What happened, what happened? Joe asked, clearly terrified. "You and your Cadillac", I said. They thought you are Immigration Officer and run away." And then he laid it on me, "How dare you bring illegals to my house, of all places." After I calmed him down, I called the guys back and everybody is laughing because Joe knew them all.

In 1974, we had another son, and named him Alexander after father. Gregory was to be named Alex and the next one if a boy, would be named Spiro after my brother, but the seer of the family, mother, prevailed, because according to her teaching, the first born has to have its own name, without any ties to a family member. Gregory was christened by Stoyan and

Miriam in the Russian Orthodox Church since we did not have a Macedonian church in the area.

When I worked at Commercial Painting in Niagara Falls, I meet a Greek co-worker by name of Kostas Cosmas, and we became lifelong friends. In the Greek tradition to be invited to be a godfather has deep meaning since it solidifies the friendship and bestows a big honor on a person. Since Stoyan christened Gregory, Kostas, the same day said to me, "For the next baby, don't look for a godfather, because you already have him, I and Jeanie (his wife) will be godparent's understand?" Of course I did. In our Orthodox religion, it is customary, if the circumstances allow that you christen babies within the first year of birth. Kostas was apolitical and I never expressed my feelings to him about Greek mistreatment of Macedonians. He and his wife, Genie were genuinely decent people and had two most adorable girls, Akrivy and Niki. One day we discussed the timing of the upcoming christening when Kostas told me that he would like to christen my son in the Greek Church. He said, "I have been member there from the beginning and attended weddings and christenings, and it would be my big honor to have a chance to christen Alex in my church in front of my few good friends and relatives." If it was anybody else, I would have dropped him like a hot potato, but Kostas was a special character. He was a very loyal friend, our religions were identical, so instead of thinking politically, I tempered my action and took the diplomatic solution and said, "let's go and do it."

My brother and family came from Toronto, my sister and her family from Ohio and my cousin Aristidi and Aunt Ristana from Youngstown also came. A few years before this, my sister had a daughter she named Aneta and we were going to see them in Lorraine often and they used to come to us and any time we were together, mother was in her glory. Those were the best years as a family with our house, our boys, and our business. And don't forget that we were very close with Bette's family. Her mother was driving and her parents would come to visit quite often. The boys were growing and it became obvious that we needed more space. The steps were getting more and more difficult for mother and going downstairs, she tripped and rolled down the hallway suffering a broken hand. Soon after, Gregory stumbled and rolled down from the top of the steps and that sped our decision.

In Orchard Park, I found a beautiful lot and bought it. I went to a draftsman who was doing other builder's plans and we designed a beautiful Mediterranean ranch style house. Since I knew by now all the contractors, and painting so many new houses, watching them being built from the beginning to the end, it was a totally fulfilling, thrilling undertaking to build my own house. The house was finished and we moved in. Our apartment I rented to a fella named Richard with the understanding that he would cut the grass and keep the driveway clean of snow. That arrangement worked much better because Richard did much more, even looking after my parents. He and his wife would check on them, bring them some groceries if they needed it, and were always reassuring me that everything was okay. And, Janet, the neighbor? Well I called her to give father the shots and she was very pleased to accommodate me. But under one circumstance: she would never accept any pay for that and despite how many times I offered to pay her, she would say, "Once more with money and I quit. Get somebody else if you want to pay." What a strange person.

As soon I moved to the new house, we parted the business relations with Joe Gialanza. The relations between builders and contractors many times is such that one month you want to strangle the builder and the next month you want to kiss him. Joe was expanding from houses only to multi-unit apartments and that takes a big investment. I used to liken myself to being the last hole in the clarinet, where the saliva spits out. I had grown the business to 20-25 employees and the cash flow has to be constant to meet not only payroll, but the 800 pound gorilla – remember? So we parted very amicably. I always appreciated that he gave me my start in the business.

The word spreads fast in any related industry, and about week later, John Marrano who lived down the street, knocks on my door. Marrano Builders was and is the biggest residential builder in WNY and is rated in the 100 biggest builders in the nation. He said, "George, I want to talk to you. I hear you are available and we like you to work with us." "Sure, why not." I answered. Mr. Marrano said, "OK, here is a telephone number, call him, his name is Gervase and you guys come to agreement." How and why, I got stuck with these Italians? Is not there some Polish contractor so we can speak Polish? Yes, there were some but, I could not communicate with them because they did not speak Polish. So I called Mr. Gervase, and I invited him for breakfast, where he outlined the expectations. I explained him that I am in painting business, not in money printing business, and I have to maintain the cash flow to keep going. We agreed on the prices for each model and just like that, we were in business. He was a young, very pleasant fellow and he helped me a lot until I situated myself in their organization.

However, I encountered some unpleasant situations in the new house in Orchard Park. Firstly, on the back of the lot there was some small creek and a large chunk of land was very muddy and wet. It was, in fact, overwhelmed with snakes. Snakes were all over the grass, the boys were unable to play outside, the neighbor had a snake in the basement and one day, when Bette was mowing the yard, a snake went inside the lawnmower and flew out in a million pieces. Secondly, some of the neighbors, the older settlers in Orchard Park, had a very snotty attitude, they thought to live in Orchard Park was some sort of entitlement and how dare we, (new residents) invade their territory, especially me with a foreign accent. To them it was like there goes the neighborhood. I did not feel comfortable at all.

By the end of the second year, Bette discreetly put an ad and a picture of the house in a specialty magazine, mostly for professional readers. So the telephone calls started coming. An elderly Croatian couple came, and they loved the house. They were examining the back yard, speaking Serbo-Croatian. They were saying, "there we will put fence, here we will make a garden, and look there is a creek to water the garden." And I understood every word, and know their plans. So they tried to gouge me on the price saying that they are going to pay cash. I told them, "I don't care how you pay, I'll get the cash anyway." The next day, another couple shows up. It was going to be a second marriage for both of them and when they saw the layout of the house, the master wing on one side and the other bedrooms opposite, perfect privacy, they made an offer right on the spot. They were 10 thousand dollars below asking price and I declined their offer because I was sure the Croatians would match the price. One questioned the other, "Honey, am I worth $5000 to you?" The answer was "Sure you are." The bride said, "Well you are worth a lot to me and I love the house so let's buy it splitting the $10,000. So they gave me $1000 non-refundable money deposit, signed a provisional contract and I submitted it to my lawyer. In about two months, the deal closed and we had doubled our money. Sure enough, the very next day the other couple called back but it was too late.

However, now we needed place to stay. Joe still owed me about $3000 and I struck a deal with him. In Lancaster, I had painted 14 buildings for him, 12 units each. I said "Joe, don't pay me the balance, let me have a place for few months and if I overstay what you owe me, I'll pay you the balance." It was okay with him. So we moved to the apartment and stayed there for seven months. In the meantime, Bette found an excellent location in town of Elma, we bought the lot and built a split level house, all in 7 months. In the spring of 1979, we moved in to the new house and that was the best decision we made. Elma is a rural community, the neighbors are all super people with children growing up and more-less the same ages, like us. No stuck up attitudes like in Orchard Park.

Business wise, we were absolutely swamped with work. I grew the company to be about the biggest in WNY for residential homes, we were spitting out between 120-150 homes a year. In the late summer, however, father's health took for the worst. The diabetes was out of control, and he had to go to the hospital again. Dr. Schultz called me to come to see him and explained that gangrene started setting on the left toe and would be progressing up the leg. He said that they would have to cut the leg, but not right way, as he had to be strengthened medically. The doctor also wanted us, his family, to talk to him and prepare him mentally, because it is a traumatic event and he might have to go to a medical nursing home. When I questioned as to when the surgery would take place he told me that they did not want to wait longer than a week. I went home to explain everything to mother, and obviously she was flabbergasted with the turn of events. I said, "Mother we can put him in the home if you can't take care of him." Her answer was, "No son, the home is out of question. I will try to take care of him, with your help taking him to the doctor's appointments. I put up all my life with your grandmother and I'll put up with him. That's my destiny from God. We ate the head of the fish and we will eat the tail." This is from the vocabulary of her wisdom bag.

The next day I took mother and went to see him. Father saw us and started crying, "now on my old age I have to be crippled, George, don't let them cut my leg. Let them leave me alone so I can die with dignity." I asked the nurse to page Dr. Schultz and in a few minutes he came. He read the mood in the room, and started talking to father, "Alex, we are on the right track now, you will have nurse coming to you house to check on you, you have many years left to live and you'll be okay." By the end of the week, I had meeting in father's room with the surgeon who will conduct the operation. He pulled some electronic scanners out and started sliding them on father's legs and said, "Listen Alex, this is the good leg and you could hear the blood flow gargling from the top to the bottom. Now the bad leg", and starts manipulating the gizmo from the top to bottom. Past the knee and in middle of the leg, the scanner started slowing and by the time it reached the end – dead silence- no blood circulation. "We have to do it tomorrow so we can save most of the leg", the doctor says and marks the spot below the knee where he suggest it be cut.

After some crying, hugging and assurances, we left father and went home. The next day the surgery went okay, but father being sedated was not responding. Before he came home, I looked a few places and bought him a new wheelchair, but after bringing it home, it would not fit into the bathroom so I had to modify the door. About week after the surgery I brought him home and trained him how to maneuver the "Cadillac" as we renamed the wheelchair. Gradually and with huge effort by mother the situation somehow stabilized except the he did not like the strict diet the Dr. prescribed. He would climb on the wheelchair and cruise through the house, like small child and yeah, it sure feels like driving a Cadillac. I am sure that he never had touched a Cadillac in his life but as long as he was happy.

In February 1980, the Winter Olympics were held in Lake Placid, NY. Obviously the most dramatic occurrence was that the US hockey team put together strictly by college kids beat the invincible Russian team assembled by strictly professionals camouflaged as soldiers. The evening of February 22nd, like most of the sports minded people in the world, I was watching the game also. It was 7:15pm when the phone rang. It was mother. She said only two words – your father – and I jumped, called the ambulance and drove to their house. As I approached the house, the ambulance was pulling up also.

Father is sprawled on the couch and the medics started working on him. "We were on the couch, watching a movie and all of the sudden he collapsed", mother said. They put him in the ambulance and drove to St. Joseph Hospital in Cheektowaga. I followed them. I was told to wait in the waiting room. The TV is blasting, a few people there are screaming from elation and the so called "Miracle on Ice" happened. The US beat the Russians. A young doctor comes in, but there is no miracle for me. "I am very sorry, the doctor says, we started the heart for about 2 minutes and then lost him. We tried everything." I asked the doctor the reason he died and he responded heart attack." I questioned if it had anything to do with his missing leg? The doctor replied, "Not whatsoever." And on that day at the age of 83, father left us. All his life struggling, hardworking, long separations from the family and now it is over.

What gives me inner satisfaction and big pride is that the last eighteen years he spent with the family, living in our home, with his grandchildren and in total happiness. The doctor offered me a sedative but I did not need it, thanked him and left. And now a new chapter starts in the life like the soap opera "As the world turns". I went to mother, explained everything to her and tried to bring her home with us. But no. Surprisingly, she took it much better than I thought, but she says that she was prepared for this because she noticed some changes in his daily behavior. She would not budge and come home with us because in her old, established bible of conduct for the next 42 days, you cannot change or rearrange anything in the house. These were the unwritten rules of her generation and everybody had to follow them. The following day, I called my brother and sister and a few other close relatives, but the procedures were directed by mother.

A few years before father died, a group of Macedonians had organized and formed a Macedonian Orthodox Church by the name Sts. Cyril & Methody. They were two brothers from Solun who spread the orthodox religion throughout Europe and wrote the Cyrillic alphabet. It was a tough going to begin a church, but the group was very focused and determined; a few people signed their homes to the bank for mortgage, bought 16 acres of land on Lake Avenue, in Hamburg and started building the church hall. When the hall was completed, they started organizing dances with Macedonian folk music and all the youth, Macedonians, Serbs, Croats, and

Bulgarians were packing the hall every month bringing in revenue. On Sundays services were performed using a provisional altar and the priest used to come every second week from Hamilton, Ontario. When weddings or funerals took place, you call Hamilton or Rochester and they would dispatch the priest. At that time, I was attending meetings there and was fully aware of the situation, but I was not active due to the delicate situation with father, who was member of MPO. This group, who were building the church, were Macedonians from Yugoslavia, where Tito was the king. The MPO organization and Tito's Yugoslavia were dedicated archenemies toward each other's philosophies. My heart was with the independents from Serbia Macedonian church which this undertaking was fitting my religious needs. Father never expressed any desire where to be buried or by what church, so I decided to bury him through the new Macedonian church. With all family present, father got the proper Orthodox blessings and services and we sent him in peace to the other world. After 42 days, we brought mother with us.

Soon after, I joined the church as a full member and when we thought that we had enough money, we started planning for the actual church building. Stoyan Boshnakov, Cvetko Fotevski and I were elected as building chairmen and the task ahead of us was, putting it charitably, enormous.

When mother came with us to live, we had to make a slight eventual change. In old country, the mother had a total control of the kitchen and was the main purveyor of food for the family (you have seen those Italian movies in black and white). Here mother is in her seventies, healthy physically and driven, driven to the point that if she has to stop a bulldozer she will. Lifetime habits, reinforced by the circumstances, don't die easily. It takes time to decompress slowly and that is what we decided. So I called her in the kitchen and with a determined but very polite voice, explained to her the differences between old country and America. The kitchen belongs to Bette. You can eat anything, everything you want. You can go with Bette shopping for the food you like and teach Bette how to cook it, and teach her the Macedonian language. But she does the cooking, not you. If you feel good, help Bette with the boys, with the laundry, or plenty of other things to do around the house. If you do feel not up to something, stay in your room and we will bring you the food. "Razbervash? Rasbervam!" (Understand?, Understood!) I felt guilty after this long conversation, that I had hurt her feelings but to the contrary, she was very relieved because her built in instinct was compelling her to do it, but her physical and mental

218

capabilities were depleted. The result? Bette can cook Macedonian dishes better than many Macedonians and can tell them the recipes in very clear understandable Macedonian language. She can converse with my relatives who don't speak English in Macedonian and I was told by a few that they thought I had married a Macedonian girl.

On Buffalo Road in Orchard Park there is a restaurant called Pappas', A well established place owned by Paul Pappas. Paul's father and my father were old friends and when I came in US, Paul was the very first person I met. Several times he came and picked me up in his flashy Oldsmobile and took me around on a discovery tour of the area. Later, when he opened the restaurant, it became a gathering point for coffee for many of us. Risto Dineff, the prankster was telling me about some Macedonian doctor who came from Toronto and has a practice in West Seneca, but did not remember his name. One evening, while we were sitting in Paul's restaurant, I was facing the door. A man enters and I experienced Eureka moment. "Naso", I asked? "George", he asked? He was Naso Dzonkovski, who I had known in Wroclav, Poland. He was two years ahead of me. And, when he graduated, we split and I never saw him again. He went to Poznan to the medical facility and this is the Macedonian doctor Risto was telling me about. Well, through time we met many, many times together and had many dinners at the local restaurants and in our homes. His congenial wife, Helen, always cracked the atmosphere if we became quiet. Helen's father in Toronto was very good friend of my brother and we always had tremendous times, especially since Naso and I always talked in Polish. When Naso and Helen were coming to our house, mother would join in conversations, and mother became Naso's patient.

Chapter VIII Back to Macedonia

The business was thriving, the boys were growing and Greg started playing soccer in Elma-Marilla league and Alex opted for baseball. I finished a coaching clinic run by a retired English professional soccer player and that enabled me to coach up to high school level but, I stuck with the little league so I could coach my sons. In Toronto, Canada, where many of the former child refugees had settled, they started organizing, and created a commission with specific goals and among other pending undertakings, they were lobbying the Greek government to let them organize a reunion of all former refugees to meet in Solun, on the account of the upcoming 40th anniversary of the exodus. My nieces, Terry and Mary, along with their husbands were heavily involved in the whole organization and periodically would notify me about upcoming dances and gatherings and we attended all of them. It gave me a chance to meet many friends from Poland and Czechoslovakia and many relatives also. And we were bracing for the reunion where we anticipated we would meet with so many friends and relatives in Greece and see for the first time our villages, and introduce my family to relatives in Nivici and Lerin. But, since the criminals never go to the scene of the crime, the Greek government never allowed it to happen. So the committee focused to organize the reunion in Skopje, Macedonia. It was planned for two years ahead in the summer of 1988. In June of 1988, Gregory was graduating from Canisius High School and Alex was preparing to follow him to the same school. Mrs. Ryan, God bless you wherever you are, I'd like to tell you that I kept my promise to you that if I have sons, they will graduate from Canisius. Following Greg's graduation ceremony, Bette and I along with Stoyan and Miriam went to celebrate in a classy restaurant and afterwards we had a huge party in our backyard with all our friends. The boys were excited to go to Europe and so was Bette who does not travel well due to motion sickness. In early July we left for Skopje for the reunion. My nieces also came along with their families.

Our kids were all together enjoying themselves and learning about other alternatives of life, other than American. Bette was there mostly as a tourist, not knowing anybody, but I was so emotionally involved, I could not contain myself. We hooked up with Vasil and he was my personal guide. I met so many people from the past and many not being able to recognize them. After all, it was 40 years ago and people change. "You see them two?" Vasil asked me pointing at two short bald guys. They are the two Sekulovski brothers. Those two brothers were from village of Grazdeno. They were older than me, husky, strong kids with full dark hair on their head and mischievous little devils. And now, they were short, bald, and timid, totally changed. We are approaching them and when they saw me, "the American", the American started hollering and they ran toward us. We started hugging, dropped a few tears from happiness, and caught up with our past. After the civil war, their father landed in Taskent and after I left Czechoslovakia for Poland, they went to Russia. But afterward, they moved to Skopje. For me, the whole reunion was one huge exhilaration with happiness and demoralizing sadness. On one side I met many of my friends who were educated, successful and healthy, and on other side many of them were in deteriorating health, a few of them had died and many of them were down on their luck and struggling economically. The promises of the past (that we choose superior system than the West has chosen) evaporated in the air and the reality set deep roots.

I asked Vasil the very first day about his father, sister and brothers. His father had died a long time ago, his brothers (which we eventually met) were still around there. And his sister Sotyrka was in a home. "What do you mean?" I asked. He answered, "She had a stroke, is incapacitated and cannot speak." I grabbed Vasil and we turned around and we went to see her.

"Will she recognize me?" He responded, "She will, her mind is OK and she can hear but can't speak." We entered a run-down semi industrial looking hallway and entered the huge room when the door was opened. I scanned the room with my eyes and spotted her, sitting in bed on the right wall side. I was approaching, with Vasil behind me and the very first instance she saw me, she started crying and saying my name in total silence. I sat next to her, we hugged and she started asking questions with her *silent sixth* instinct. Vasil, who read her well, was translating my questions and I was talking to her directly. She wanted to know about mother, and some other friends, if we hang out together, if I am married and children, and so on. Back in Poland she had been taking care of all four brothers and her father, since their mother had died years ago. When I was leaving her, she was smiling, crying and hugged me, like her brother, as she treated me like one when we were in Poland. When we returned home, Bette and I went to the stores shopping and sent her plenty of essentials like robes, sleepers, socks, sweaters, pajamas. Three years later, I went back to Skopje to see my sister Todora, and the very first thing I told Vasil was that I wanted to go and see his sister. But this time the cruelty of the sickness was faster than my trip, because she had died the previous year. It broke my heart the first visit and

224

repeated itself the second time. She was a beautiful person in her early forties before she had chance to get married and become mother to enlighten the lives of her children, and she has left us in great sadness.

The first week stay in Skopje passed, with the activities, meeting friends and relatives. My sister, Todora, was also with us all week, she lives in the city of Prilep, about two hours drive away. The second week we spend in Ohrid, an old historic city with old historic monasteries of religious significance to the Macedonian Archdiocese. And also tourist attraction with Lake Ohrid beaches, which are like a magnet to German and other westerners. The third week a compulsory visit in Greece, Lerin, Nivicy and obviously Orovo. We had made arrangements back home for a rental car with air conditioning through Helen, Naso's wife, who owned travel agency. But arranging and getting it are two different things to a local travel agents, unless it happens by luck.

The weather was stifling, the temperatures hovered over 100 degrees every day, with no air in the car, but when going gets tough, the tough got to suffer. We reached the border crossing to Greece, with heavy traffic ahead of us, but thankfully we had plenty of bottled water. The boys would pour a whole water bottle on their heads and it would dry in ten minutes.

225

Finally, after about an hour and a half, we passed customs and headed to Solun. And I saw a huge sign welcoming us to Greece in Greek and English. What an irony, 40 years ago we were unceremoniously kicked out of our houses and now we are returning back as a tourist to prop up the Greek economy. The nieces with their families followed, but we got separated at the border. Our destination point was the hotel King Alexander. As soon we entered the hotel, we felt like we found an oasis in the desert. The rooms were fully air conditioned. The boys were hungry, so we ordered something to eat through room service, which in Yugoslavia they had not heard yet what that is. But in Solun, it was a metabolizing adjustment remedy. A cold bottle of Heineken will do it, instead of the foamy lukewarm beers in Skopje.

After staying overnight in Solun, a convoy of 3 cars, us and Terry and Mary's families started driving toward our village, about 2 and a half hours drive. Terry's George knew the area well and he was the lead car and we followed. We reached Lerin and headed straight to Nivicy, where I have big family of cousins, aunts and so on. Nivicy, I remember quite well, and had stayed there many times at grandmother's house, where mother comes from. From Lerin to Nivicy is about 60 kilometers of narrow, winding road, going through the mountains of Bigla and driving and looking around the landscape, everything started coming back to me, I started remembering the villages we passed, anticipated the next turns on the road, like I was absent only for a week or so, although 40 years had passed since. We went to my cousin's house, where everybody was waiting for us and cousin George looked great since he had left Poland.

The next day we went to Orovo, my village. But sadly, except for the church, the village does not exist at all. Every house is torn down. I pointed out to Bette and the boys where our house was and where our relatives used to live. The school and so on. But if you did not know it, you would never think that once upon a time, there was a vibrant, active community, full of hopes and aspirations. A paved road was leading to Grazdeno, but none of the original settlers live there. The village is occupied by resettled traveling nomads, gypsies and rejects from other Greek territories. We tried to open and see the church but was locked. So we drove to Grazdeno and located the priest who came with us and opened the door. In this church, St. Nicholas, I was christened and for eight years I was attending services with mother, played in the yard, rolled eggs at Easter, and attended many happy and sad occasions. Now abandoned, and deteriorated, with broken windows, big holes in the roof, and battered by the elements. The authorities in charge of religious objects have a difficult decision to make, you can't tear it down because we are Christian people, loving, with God-fearing religion, which would preserve religious objects, but on the other hand, we are not going to spend money for securing this religious jewel and perpetuating the existence of a Macedonian minority. That's why we populated Grazdeno with strange people, so we can lie to the world and say, "see, real Greek people live here, since we brought them here.

The priest turned out to be from the village of German, spoke fluent Macedonian, because he was Macedonian and when told him my name, turns out he knows my father by name. We looked at the magnificent icons (a display of saints in front of the altar) – and the memories started overwhelming me. There are the steps to the upper floor, I carefully climb up, against urging of the priest not to, for safety reasons. We picked up some debris from the floor and snapped a bucket of pictures. On the side of the altar are a few icons, and I asked the priest if I could buy one to take home. "No, he responds, it is illegal to take historic items out of the country, if they catch you at the border, you will go to jail." It makes sense. I took one small stone from where our house was and a lone roofing tile from the church. Back home, I restored the tile, framed it and is hanging in my house with a huge picture of the the church. We visited with family the rest of the day and next morning left for Prilep, where my sister lives. The time went fast, and after 4 weeks of an unforgettable vacation, we came home.

Soon after, I started a fundraiser among our people from Orovo to secure the integrity of the church. We are spread between a few states and Canada, and I sent to everybody from Orovo, a picture of the exterior of the church and letter of explanation. I had estimated (based on the value of the dollar) that the improvements would cost about $9000. Mother warned me that I committed myself to the cause and if there is shortage of money, I have to make up the difference, of which I was fully aware and prepared. The donations started coming and soon I had in the account $13,000. I went back to Greece, hired a civil engineer, went to the church side, he saw what is needed and gave me a professional blueprint of proceedings. The irony is that he was real Greek and would not accept any compensation for his services due to the fact that it is a Christian church. Then he hooked me up with a builder who also was decent person and came with me to the church to see the needs, although he knew the church.

We also needed permission from the bishop in Lerin and the bishop needs permission from the religious section of the state in Athens, which would take a day or two. The builder gave me a written

estimate with all stipulations to be met for about ten
to eleven thousand dollars. I would leave the money
with my nephew in Nivici, and he, an established
business man, with a restaurant and hotel, would pay
the builder in increments as the job progressed.
Agreed and signed. We go to see the Bishop of Lerin
and he has the OK from Athens. He questioned "Who
is going to do the work?" "Me, your Excellency", replied
the builder. The bishop, "How much is the work
worth?" The reply was about $11,000. Again the
bishop, "Who done the drawings?" The reply was
"Mister XXXXX " (I could kick myself not remembering
the names). The civil engineer, and I showed him the
paperwork. "How are you going to get paid?", the
bishop asked. "His nephew will have the money." "No,
it does not work that way, the bishop says, with
irritation in his voice. Our estimates are for $18,000,
and the money in full amount has to be delivered to us,
so we will commence the payment to be assured that
the job is done correctly. IT is our responsibility." "If it
is your responsibility, how come you let the building
deteriorate to such level?, I asked. You don't care the
church is abandoned, inactive, the village does not
exist and we from outside the country want to preserve
it for posterity." I could see sparks shooting form his
eyes and smoke coming from his nostrils, his face
reddened but he controlled himself and said if we want

to do something about the church, that is the only way. We don't let foreigners dictate how to run our country. I left and ran to my cousin Politimia and called my brother in Toronto. "Did you give him any money?", my brother asks. "No!" "Good leave the place, and under no circumstances give the bishop any money, because you are not going to see the money ever and they won't do anything to fix the church." There are people from another village, Ostima, and happened to them the same thing except they lost $30,000. So what kind of leverage did I have with the bishop, who is part of the corrupted, politically inspired conspiracy? None. So I came home to a big disappointment to my mother, and wrote another letter with explanation to all donors and refunded their money back.

Speaking about churches, we were tremendously successful with building of our church. Stoyan, Cvetko and I got great cooperation from the Macedonian Community and many dedicated individuals went beyond their capabilities to work, to donate, and to help in any capacity they could. There were few malcontents who disagreed with this or that, without having their own solution to a problem, but complain or oppose that very important cause, it means you must have been born as a breech baby, and nothing will satisfy you. In the summer of 1984, the bishop in charge of the American-Canadian diocese from Skopje, Macedonia, His Excellency Bishop Kiril, came and officially consecrated the church at front of a huge crowd. The church is for us a huge magnet that draws people not only for Sunday and holiday services but for all kind of occasions, wedding, christenings, private parties and services for the people who God called back.

From the business end, Colony Painting and Wall Covering was prospering well, for every account we drop or they kick us out, we get new accounts and at that time, we were servicing Forbes Homes, which was run by three totally unusual partners, who were astonishing me in every aspect on a daily basis. Mr. Harry Schmitt and Mr. David Blitzer are survivors of the German labor camps during the second World War, they are Polish Jews and we would always speak in Polish. The third partner was the son of a friend of Harry's & David's, a much younger educated lawyer, his name was Elliot Lasky. They ran the business informally, never hiding behind the secretaries and always available if something went wrong. I could swear at them in Polish and nobody else would understand it. Elliot was slightly on the aloof side, maybe due to the age difference, but all three were straight and honest to the core. Once we agreed on prices or any conditions, our word was more binding than signed contract which we never had signed. Elliot was minding the sales and technical aspects of the business, David dealt with banks and closings and Harry was the money man, billings, checks, contractors, etc.

In the winter of 1985, I had a knee surgery which put me out of circulation for about 3 months. Any time I was gone, my faithful foremen John Durphy was running the business. I stopped in the office, still on crutches to see them. Both David and Harry individually called me in their offices and offered me any amount of loans at no interest to pay my medical bills. Thankfully, I was insured and did not need money, but think, only old world people think that way. They were unusual in many ways, in their demeanor, and in their way of talking to people. I spent many years working for Forbes Homes and I became very comfortable to the point that I started thinking like I am sort of part owner. I started doing all sorts of extra-curricular activities like picking up sheets of plywood and lumber if they were exposed to the weather elements. Closing the doors and windows and telling my employees to do the same thing and many, many times, Harry would consult me about some obnoxious customers and I would stick my nose in to help him.

There was a customer who worked for Ford Motor Company, who became sort of benign terrorist. Every time he would enter the building, which was almost every morning, the girls in the room would run to avoid him. And when he started complaining about the fireplace mantle, having natural grain on the front, Elliott had called me to meet him the next morning in the office. Ford was celebrating their 75th anniversary and it was all over in the newspapers. And there was also a note that they are recalling about seven thousand Ford vehicles for some malfunction. I cut and took the paper with me.

The next morning, I entered Elliott's office and he is already there. I asked, "What is the problem

Elliott?" Elliott replied, "He does not like the look of the mantle." And I turned toward the customer and said. "Look, I did not make the wood, I stained it, sealed it, sanded it, and varnished it. Did I done a good job?" "Yes", he answered. So I said, "Now, from what I can see the carpenter did excellent job balancing the plywood to look proportionate on both ends. Wait, wait, I am talking now. People pay big money to get such a nice grainy look, you got lucky, got that for free. If you don't like the grain, then I will paint it. And you are building a house in January in Buffalo weather, and constantly complaining. By the time you move in the new house you will hate it. Besides, what kind of work you are doing?" "I work for Ford", he responds. And I pull out the newspaper and tell him that Ford, after 75 years, still builds crap autos and I am only a painter, not a psychiatrist and left the office. An hour later, Elliot calls me on the cell phone. "Georgio, I was so proud of you, you put him on the spot. And you can do it but I can't talk that way to the clients." On many occasions, Harry was using me as a trouble shooter. Once a garage door panel had a hole in the middle and I knew who done it; the plumber had backed in his van into it. Harry got estimates from the door people for about $400. But I said, "Harry, let me try it first, maybe I can fix it. And I fixed it."

Harry comes, looks and cannot tell where was the hole. "Good job George, saved me $400" and he gave me $20 bill, saying "here take your wife for lunch". "Harry", I said, "my wife does not go to McDonalds for lunch, pull out some more." Feeling slightly embarrassed, (Harry embarrassed? No) he took the $20 back and gave me $100 bill. So then I say, "No Harry it is too much, give me only $50". (I hope my wife does not read this because I never took her to lunch.)

In the winter of 1985, we and Stoyan with Miriam had gone to Acapulco on vacation. It was one of the best vacations ever. Stoyan and I tried waterskiing and the girls parasailing. The girls shopped and Stoyan and I ate lots of fish. Miriam would say she needs to buy a dress and Stoyan would say when I married you, you only had one dress and only twenty years later you have 100% more and still need more? For Christmas he had bought her a diamond ring but kept it quiet from me. I learned it from Bette. At dinner I teased him how big a diamond it is and he says one carat. I say "That's all you, you cheapskate?" So he countered, " What did you buy Bette?" I bragged, "I bought her a full set of Tupperware, which is much bigger than your measly diamond." And everybody would laugh. We were loud on purpose. Those were the best times.

236

Some time later, Stoyan got sick and the diagnosis was grim. Cancer of the stomach. After surgery and treatments he went into remission and the life became good again. So to celebrate the good outcome and thinking how of the good times we had few years a back in Acapulco, we decided to go back there. We stayed at the same hotel, had great food, went to see the cliff divers but, the novelty had worn out from the previous trip. Lo and behold the sickness came back and after a valiant struggle, Stoyan died in May 1990 at the age of 52. Our normal life was upset to the maximum, my sons went through difficult time and to this day both of them talk about, remember and miss Uncle Stoyan. On the positive side, he saw the marriage of his daughter, Maritza to a terrific fellow, Jack Ruh, before he died. Jack and Maritza have 8 children, 6 girls and 2 boys who are the most grounded, level headed and well behaved kids I know and Stoyan would have been very proud had he lived. The girls names I know but cannot tell who is who because they all look so much alike, but the boys are Jack and Stoyan. However Stoyan's younger brother, Vancho and his wife Zora, stepped in and are doing a tremendous job of taking care of the children and helping Maritza in any way possible. Once I took 4 of them for lunch and by the time I brought them home, I was totally exhausted. So I give big kudos to Vancho and Zora.

Soon after Stoyan died, mother started complaining. But crying so many times wolf, we thought it is nothing unusual. But few days later, she shows me her stomach is bloated with fluids and I call Naso. He admitted her to Mercy Hospital and after few weeks of treatments, he stabilized her. She needed constant medical maintenance and shots, so he kept her as long as the rules allowed, then switched her in the nursing wing. Between Bette and I, we saw her everyday and except for retaining fluids, she was, most of the time, in good spirits.

One Sunday at noon, I go to see her as Naso is leaving, we met in the hallway. Naso is laughing, "your mother scolded me", he says. "Why? Because I was dressed in sport shirt with short sleeves. "You are not golf player, she said, with short sleeves, you are a doctor so dress properly". Eventually they discovered colon cancer and had to do a second surgery. She struggled, complained, and worried about her grandsons, her mind was always fixed on the well being of the boys. The sickness ran its course and in September 1993, she left us. After father's problems we went through similar situations with Bette's parents and now mother had joined them in the Garden of Eden. And when I look back through all the obstacles, wars, hardship, sicknesses, separations, all sorts of agonizing, mother was the constant that kept us all together, who nourished our souls, who cooled us when we would get hot and who warmed us when we were cold. And now she is gone. But through life, she was teaching us what is right, saturated us with her wisdom and showed us how to persevere in difficult times. Because now that I am mature, the father of two wonderful sons and two little granddaughters, I feel confident if I can pass on to them at least part of what I learned from mother, they are going to be all right.

Epilogue: Where are they now?

It started as an aberration of the norm. A stupid, ill thought, ill-conceived operation to save the children from the fallout of the war, which they started, in order to satisfy their egos and the megalomaniacs of a few incorrigible revolutionists that were under spell of communist ideology which in turn was mostly influenced by the Russians and specifically, the biggest butcher in history, Joseph Stalin. I don't know much about the children in other countries like Romania or Hungary, so I will stick with Poland and Czechoslovakia. Many of us, who were lucky to have relatives in the USA, Canada, or Australia, wound up in those countries. Many of us, who had parents in Greece, went there. Many of us married local girls and are still in Poland or Czechoslovakia. Many, from the beginning, went to Bulgaria. But the most, I think found themselves in Macedonia. Many, many of them went to universities, became engineers, doctors (Naso for example), technocrats, and in Macedonian field, held many important positions in the industries.

Also a few of us, due to the difficulties of coping with the reality or personal predisposition wound up in the gutter of life. For many of us, achieving the success of education was the salvation which we would never have had chance in Greece. Many of us just plainly got lost in the environment of daily life and could not give two cents, happy-go-lucky into oblivion. But the tragedy lies in the fact that many of us did not have the chance to go back or to see their parents or relatives again. The parents would die from broken hearts, not seeing their children again, notwithstanding the fact that the little boy or girl is now educated person. And the Greek government most of the time being lead by western educated leaders still adheres to the cruel and inhumane principal that it does not issue visas to anybody who was born in Macedonia or goes by their Macedonian name. They were snatched from their parents as kids, their parents died in the villages, leaving all the properties.

And the legitimate children are not allowed to go and light a candle on their parents' graves. So this is how the people who brought to the world centuries ago the knowledge, the architecture, the math, the medicine and the word "democracy" treat their children and their parents. They terrorize legitimate minorities in their own place of birth. A glorious history of the past is being eroded by small minds, who run the present day Greece. Shame.

Made in United States
Orlando, FL
28 March 2022